Light for the Dark Side:

Ethics Cases for University Administrators

by

Dr. J. Thomas Whetstone

DORRANCE
PUBLISHING CO
EST. 1920
PITTSBURGH, PENNSYLVANIA 15238

Dorrance Publishing Co
585 Alpha Drive
Pittsburgh, PA 15238
Visit our website at *www.dorrancebookstore.com*

ISBN: 978-1-4809-8748-7
eISBN: 978-1-4809-8863-7

Dedication

In memory of Professor Kenneth Madison McDonald, Ph.D., my beloved grandfather. He taught me to read and then to love to read. A great teacher who was ever popular with his students, at the depths of the Great Depression he lost his contract at a major university after refusing to change the grade of a football player.

Contents

Preface

This book is written in the belief that Christian college and university administrators should, and can, be excellent educators and leaders. For this they are to practice a God-honoring ethic. Empowered and called by the Holy Spirit, Christian administrators should outshine others, faithfully and optimistically seeking to be ethical exemplars in the fallen world.

Christian colleges and universities are dedicated to shining as lights of God's Kingdom in their communities and throughout the created world. Their faculties, staff, and administrators are privileged to serve Christ-centered missions: propagating the gospel, educating future servant leaders for the church and for God-honoring vocations, and promoting a sanctified vision of social culture. Christian institutions thus are to be different from public and other secular universities. Their distinctives result in substantive marketing niches, but it is much more than that.

This sacred obligation grows more critical and more challenging as the overall moral fabric of American society abandons its Judeo-

Christian heritage. However, in spite of their public persona and public relations claims, do those who lead Christian institutions in the twenty-first century still possess zeal for the service they espouse? Or have they somehow become lukewarm, seeing their positions as just stops on a career path? Do administrators look on faculty and staff as components of an impersonal organization, disposable parts that can be replaced when worn down or imperfectly fitting the latest agenda? Are faculty members rewarded primarily for their personal research successes? When pressed by donating parents, do administrators encourage faculty members to inflate or even change student grades?

What is the central driving force for administrators? Do financial pressures lead them to add or delete programs for short-term, pragmatic reasons—rather than making decisions based on prayerful strategic planning grounded in a consensual commitment to the long-term mission for education of their students? Do administrators rationalize hard budget and personnel decisions as being necessary to support the Christian mission and the very existence of the institution, when they may actually be driven more by their own agendas and career progress? When finances are tight—seemingly the normal status for Christian institutions—do administrators see this also as an opportunity to cut or dispose of people who might present a competitive threat to their agendas? Do institutional policies and their enforcement in areas such as gender equality, employment rights, and compensation match or fall short of industry standards? Or are faculty and staff expected to sacrifice because of their commitment to Christian service, while the institution is sheltered from government intervention by its Christian identity? Do administrators relate to outside contractors, consultants, and adjunct instructors professionally and fairly, without engaging in conflicts of interest?

Does the actual as well as the publicized culture promote speaking the truth with love? Do all possess and perceive an institution-wide culture of honesty and trust? Or do faculty consider administrators as being on the Dark Side while administrators see at least some faculty as too much devoted to their self-interests?

Surely most administrators and faculty who consider the above questions should be encouraged that they can answer the majority, if not all, favorably for themselves and their institutions. Moreover, they understand that until Christ returns there will be no ideal social body, even a local church or Christian university. Nevertheless, students, alumni, trustees, and all other constituents are entitled to expect a sanctified ethical witness from Christian administrators and faculty members.

This book includes some specific cases based on actual situations that suggest some of the above questions. The author attempts to offer realistic scenarios while avoiding any identification of actual people, institutions, or times. The aim is to encourage thoughtful reading and discussion to help people prepare for times when they will encounter similar ethical challenges and temptations. Christian presidents, deans, faculty, and students can become even more ethically sensitive and better prepared to engage their daily responsibilities for the glory of the Lord. Perfection is beyond us all, but we all can strive to improve by the grace of God. We can be optimistic that He will grant us success.

J. Thomas Whetstone, D.Phil.
708 Sarasota Arch
Chesapeake, VA, USA
twhetstone1@cox.net

January 2019

Acknowledgments

I could never have completed this book without the encouragement and support of my beloved wife, Nancy, who also served magnificently as my principal editor. I also commend Dean Beth Doriani for her insightful comments on the cases as well as her example as an excellent Christian academic administrator. Dean Stanley Baczek of Cedarville University graciously allowed three of his cases to be included.

Chapter One

Introduction

Faculty who accept appointments as deans are sometimes accused of changing sides, going over to the "dark side," thus being perceived as tragic traitors like Darth Vader of *Star Wars*. In her contribution to *The Ethical Challenges of Academic Administration*, Donna Werner (2010, p. 37) relates that she detected a new trace of animosity in the comments of colleagues after becoming an interim dean, and she soon learned that her decisions could make her quite unpopular. "Despite one's best intentions, on most days, there will be at least one faculty member who is angry with decisions made by his dean" (Werner, 2010, p. 47). She was especially troubled because she expected to return to a faculty role after her interim appointment. The narrow way required to avoid conflicts of interest is especially treacherous for interims.

Perceptions of administrators as constituting a dark side are not exclusive to secular campuses. The central normative proposition of this book is that Christian administrations and faculties need to overcome the good side versus dark side social phenomenon. This requires Christian leaders of strong moral character who seek to develop virtuous organizations that have a strong culture organized around a godly mission (Whetstone, 2013, 2017). Administrators, faculty, and staff must respond to a genuine sense of calling to serve Christ. However, animosities between and among faculty and administrators still seem to well up and fester. When these Manichean-like phenomena occur, the board and administrators, and the members of faculty, should feel obligated to find out why and seek spiritual, educational, and administrative remedies.

The Representative Cases

This author does not attempt to propose a utopian solution for this particular social aspect of the Fall. Perfect harmony is an unrealistic ideal prior to Christ's return in glory. This book therefore merely breaches an uncomfortable subject, offering a selection of cases based on problematic situations and decisions that have occurred in Christian academic contexts. These cases are gathered from a multitude of institutions and employ fictional names. The intent is to highlight ethical issues that thoughtful readers and discussants can analyze. It is hoped that these representative case situations will serve to alert and encourage Christian administrators and faculty as they grow in their sanctification as practicing academics.

Chapter three presents a basic model for ethical decision-making that can guide case analysis and discussion. The cases in this volume are not unsolvable quandaries but are meant to be realistic challenges that can require recognizing complex realities including the histories behind the situations, personal interrelationships, and conflicting pressures faced by those involved.

Serious, thoughtful discussion of the ethical challenges facing Christian academic leaders is not merely an academic exercise but is itself an ethical obligation. Constituents and broader society expect Christian college and university leaders to be moral exemplars—arguably holding them to even higher standards than increasingly are applied to corporate leaders (see Paine, 2003). Many Christian institutions require employees to sign statements agreeing with faith positions; however, an organization of righteous people is not enough to guarantee righteous or virtuous organizational decisions in the reality of fallen internal and external contexts. The right organizational structures also need to be put in place, and decision makers need to have positive support from superiors and other organizational members to make and implement wise judgments ethically.

Constituents can recognize moral failure either in individual faculty or administrators or by the institution as a collective identity. Students are especially quick to respond when ethically questionable policies, such as sudden elimination of promised majors or classes, affect them. They learn unintended lessons that can harden their sensibilities and undermine their trust in the school. Whereas the personification of institutions is ontologically problematic, it nevertheless can be useful to take a metaphorical approach of envisioning the Christian academic institution as an actor subject to a biblical ethic. Leaders can use a virtuous organization metaphor to envision and communicate the values, normative intent, and policies of the institutional culture in pursuit of its overall mission. Such focused effort is what constituents expect. Walking the talk is obligatory.

Some administration actions are more noticeable than others. For example, when respected professors, whose contracts are not renewed for budgetary reasons, are escorted by uniformed guards from their offices to assure that they leave the campus, students and other faculty are appalled. The university's policy might be legal, but treating faculty as criminals is not ethical. Administrators should seek justice and speak the truth with love (Eph 4:15), building rather than undermining a culture of trust.

Many of the ethical issues that face academic administrators involve employee relationships such as hiring decisions and processes, load balancing and course scheduling, compensation, conflict management, performance reviews, committee assignments, travel authorization and expense reimbursement, research support, promotion and tenure, and termination policy. Particularly difficult are questions of conflict of interest, nepotism, and student and faculty grievances. Communication failures instigate and can exacerbate issues of almost any type. One of the representative cases addresses relationships with an outside consultant.

Avoiding or even recognizing conflicts of interest can be difficult. A lack of integrity is shown when a dean terminates her assistant without warning by email from out of town, especially if she acts in order to make the position available for a family friend (Curren, 2010). Even if the action were justified, it is incumbent on the dean to explain such a decision face-to-face; not doing so manifests a lack of courage. Neither is it ethically reasonable for an incoming president to terminate or demote a provost or dean merely to make room for a friend. Both cases involve a conflict of interest with potential harm to the good of the institution.

Nepotism is often banned by a university's policy because it is blatantly impartial and unfair and thus harmful to a culture of openness, fairness, and trust. But nepotism has prevailed at some important Christian universities, at least in the uncontested practice of passing on top leadership posts from father to son. This is especially problematical if nepotism is prohibited by policy for employees other than those in the founder's immediate family.

Communication practice is also a major category of ethical concern. For example, it is unethical for chairs to lie to faculty about their poor performance so as not to discourage them (Kline, 2010). "White lies" meant to maintain department morale fail to treat faculty with due respect. They instead undermine a commitment to the pursuit and dissemination of truth.

A university president who misleads his board of trustees about enrollment or revenues also exhibits a failure of integrity. Such dishonesty takes on special institutional significance when it is material to the board's oversight and the president has a responsibility to disclose matters material to that oversight (Curren, 2010, p. 69). The board of trustees also has a moral obligation to monitor properly the president's reports, establishing ways to audit institutional performance and to verify information provided. A board that allows the president to be its only source of information, as in the case of the president allowing no other institutional member to answer questions from the board at a meeting without his prior review, is also derelict in its role responsibilities to the institution.

The following cases only begin to address the totality of situations and issues that administrators and faculty face. For example, sexual harassment is not featured as an aspect in any of the cases although this vicious behavior is receiving great attention at this time. This multifaceted plague perhaps deserves attention in another volume. The cases included herein do highlight some important examples of the issues outlined above, raising representative concerns in each of three key interrelated components of a virtuous organization: mission, culture, and leadership (Whetstone, 2005b). Readers might well identify additional ethical challenges based on their diverse expertise and experiences. And the preferred solutions for the case situations may vary, depending on the environmental and cultural context, the institutional mission, and the nature of the people involved. Good solutions do exist, and Christian leaders should carefully select and implement them with proper humility and an attitude of forgiveness.

This book of cases and its several essays is being published as a resource for the development of current and future leaders of academic institutions. The cases represent the diversity of ethical challenges that presidents, provosts, deans, and department chairs regularly face. Anyone, from students to trustees and other governing authorities, donors, leaders of other organizations, and members of the general public impacted by the leadership examples and contributions of academic institutions—just about everyone in our society—hopefully also can learn and profit from the light shed from discussion and thoughtful efforts to resolve the issues raised.

Chapter Two

Organizational Mission, Culture, and Leadership

How can the leaders of a university or college establish an ethical organization? This is a vitally important challenge for the board of trustees and administrators. They must structure their efforts realistically given the issues and trends in the external environment. They also must assure that the organizational ethic conforms to and supports the theological grounding, strategic direction, and constituencies of the institution.

Internal assessment and any revamping of the institution's collective ethics approach should concentrate on institutional mission, culture, and leadership—basic components of any ethical organization (see Whetstone, 2005b). These structural components are intertwined. The culture, being organized by the mission and an essential factor in its accomplishment, is a primary concern of institutional leaders. Each of these components is elaborated below to provide a broader organizational context and perhaps promote deeper and more practical discussion of the issues and possible solutions for the selected cases that represent some of the ethical situations that confront Christian administrators.

Mission

One of the key ethical considerations for academic administrators at any level must be the mission of the institution (Englehardt et al., 2010, p. xvi). Mission statements of American colleges and universities typically include two common elements: (1) to develop and nurture a community of scholars in order to advance human knowledge; and (2) to develop and nurture a community of learners, in order to develop the individual and make good citizens (ibid.). An academic institution should address each of these elements in its mission. Because a Christian college's mission is spiritual as well as academic, it should also express its spiritual commitment to equip students for service in their Christian callings.

Administrators charged with making strategic and operational decisions need to have appropriate conceptual knowledge and willful commitment to the institution's academic excellence, as defined by its avowed mission, purpose, and goals. Ethical integrity, mission, and basic values need to inform all decisions, plans, policies, procedures, programs, and activities. This goes beyond mere compliance to legal and assessment requirements (see Paine, 1994).

The president has a fundamental responsibility for maintaining and enhancing the integrity and character of the institution and for representing the institution and its students, faculty, staff, alumni, board, and other constituencies with strong moral and ethical values (Romesburg, 2008). The mission statement can be an effective tool when it clearly communicates and guides institutional actions and when administration and faculty at every level commit to achieving its aims. On the other hand, vague mission statements and publicity documents that celebrate "excellence" and "leadership for worldwide change" merely gloss over a fragmentation (and fogging over) of purpose if the colleges do not offer a viable road map for achieving that end and give administrators a method for implementing and assessing programs devoted to it (Donovan, 2010).

For the Christian academic institution, decision makers at every level need to have a strong spiritual aspiration to promote the integration of Christian faith and learning. This starts with a genuine sense of calling to nurture a Christ-centered, Spirit-led culture throughout the institution. Any hope of success requires humility and obedience to God's scriptural revelation, faith in Christ, and trust in the priority of seeking the guidance of the Holy Spirit. Furthermore, the administrative leaders should openly encourage and support each member of the administration, faculty, and staff to exercise moral imagination in carrying out organizational responsibilities and creating ways to enhance mission performance. This suggests that a top-down, command-control approach can be counter-productive, especially when it is implemented through a bureaucratic, non-participatory organizational model.

Weingartner (1999, p. 98) observes that "the ethos of a college or university is perhaps expressed even more distinctly not by what is done there, but how things are done." The mission, purpose, and basic values need to permeate all policies, decisions, and actions, or they might be perceived as merely "window dressing." Any deficiency can even deter student learning. For example, when students in ethics courses perceive that administrators or faculty apply educational policies inconsistently or contrary to the moral stance proclaimed in the institution's mission statement, they might well respond cynically. If the institution acts pragmatically, students can reasonably question not only the value of the mission statement but also the need for an ethics course or even the practical worth of ethical analysis.

Deviations from the letter and spirit of the mission statement are risky. As assessment bodies try to emphasize, the stated mission is no less than a sacred ethical obligation. Ethicist Ron Duska (2008) claims that any organization or institution that acts apart from its mission, purpose, and basic values is corrupt. For instance, a college administration that places its primary emphasis on financial profit, recruiting aggressively for growth in student numbers while cutting costs by increasing teacher loads, freezing salaries, and cutting benefits, is risking such corruption. The trustees and administrators must act for the financial integrity of the institution, but they still must guard against compromising the academic and spiritual aspects of its mission.

None of the cases in this volume specifically focus on the adoption or assessment of an institution's mission. And while cases are not institution-specific, this does not imply that mission is anything but the proper starting point for institutional ethics. Trustees and administrators should assure that their institution's mission, purpose, and values are properly formed and communicated to ground and establish the basic context for addressing the ethical situations or issues that administrators and faculty face. Case discussants may find value in assessing the ethical choices of the case protagonists in terms of the specific mission statement of their own institutions. In some cases, this may result in different solution choices.

To exercise good judgment in searching for and implementing a decision ethically, administrators must have an understanding of the special culture and history of the institution, as well as an accurate view of the situation. Good judgment (practical wisdom or *phronesis*) also requires avoidance of conflicts of interest, maintenance of good channels of communication, awareness of relevant moral considerations, and a proper decision-making approach. Christian administrators should fulfill their organizational roles (which they are especially called by God to do) according to the excellencies of Christ.

Culture

What should be the ethical culture for a Christian university? What basic values are needed to guide the daily decisions and actions of its members in their institutional relationships and responsibilities? Institutional members must reach a consensual agreement as to their best answers. Utopian approaches are not advised, as tragic results at American secular universities sometimes demonstrate. (See, for example, an analysis of the cultural decay of the University of California (Kennedy, 2017).) Christian institutions have spiritual resources to call upon, but the challenge is a difficult one.

When a Manichean, or a "good side versus dark side" or "us versus them," mentality arises in an avowedly Christian academic institution, it should be overcome by faculty and administration genuinely seeking to walk in faith according to a biblical ethic. This is basically what institutional missions proclaim to constituencies and the general public and what their administrations and faculties owe to their callings. This requires maintaining a culture built among believers guided by a biblical decision-making ethic. It involves speaking the truth in love (Eph 4:15a).

However, whereas numerous Christian universities tout servant leadership, they too often reward the opposite. Donovan (2010) refers to "rock star" faculty who often serve their own ends rather than that of the university. A celebrity culture stresses the postmodern importance of public image, hardly a value consistent with servant leadership. Of course, a Christian university or a secular one might well point to its "superstars" as evidence of its excellence. But immoderate stress on the achievements of only a few celebrities can demoralize teachers working in the trenches with their students. Faculty and staff observe any major reductions in teaching loads and committee responsibilities for certain individuals and are well aware of who is featured in institutional journals and promotional materials. The cultural message should not be that an individual will remain second-rate unless he shifts his focus to achieving outside accolades.

Ideally, cultural values, the *via affirmativa* for the university as an organization, should be biblically-derived. Its members should strive to live, make decisions, and implement actions following the two Great Commandments, the Golden Rule, and the explicit moral authority of the Ten Commandments. The intent to treat every person impartially, as a creature made in God's image and thus worthy of dignity and respect—regardless of organizational status or other conditions—is basic. Believers should do justice, love mercy, walk humbly with the Lord (Mic 6:8), and imitate Christ, applying the question "What would Jesus do?" as a useful heuristic. Another helpful rule of thumb is the "Newspaper Principle" or *Wall Street Journal* Principle: before acting, each person should consider whether she would want her action reported in the press, where those people she most values would likely find out about it.

But faculty-administration adversarialism is ubiquitous on campuses (Newton, 2010, p. 99), and educators can face complex, often messy, challenges that require more than adherence to formulas or rules of thumb. Faculty members might say, "Just let me teach and you worry about the rest." But at other times, they might express their desire for a participative role in campus decisions. Administrators might not be comfortable with the delays participative management entails, especially resenting faculty protests concerning simple decisions clearly in the administrative jurisdiction. For example, faculty members might protest the provost's decision to terminate a poorly performing staff member who happens to be a friend of some faculty. Or the faculty might object to the way a dean seeks to reorganize her own staff. These cases become especially trying when the president or provost is easily swayed by certain faculty members, who are then encouraged to go over their dean's head on a regular basis, disrupting any sense of a proper line of authority.

In some institutions, faculty members at times are relied upon to serve part-time in administrative roles or are elevated to positions of dean or provost or even college president. And presidents and deans sometimes return to full-time faculty positions or at least regularly teach classes. Such practices should build greater understanding and appreciation of the differing challenges that confront the administration and the teaching and research scholars. However, such organizational fluidity does not necessarily eliminate the perception of some that the individuals who switch roles effectively change sides, especially when they make unpopular decisions.

Newton (2010) actually sees the administration-faculty adversarialism as good, being a social phenomenon with which faculty and administration can sometimes learn to live peaceably. She calls for better mutual understanding of the causes of the tensions, which flow according to one of the following hypotheses: (1) the two-culture hypothesis, and (2) the existence of two different and incompatible views of the university, the corporate and college models.

The two-culture hypothesis is based upon the reality that faculty work mostly with other faculty whereas administrators work with other administrators. These two groups have different hours, dress codes, and interests. Problems between them stem from a lack of mutual understanding. Moreover, boards and administrations in non-profit organizations deliberate carefully and appropriately to arrive at decisions, which they expect to be carried out, because they consider the time for questions to be over. In contrast, academic faculties seek a culture in which all decisions, conclusions, and assertions of any kind are always questioned—nothing is ever beyond inquiry. According to Newton, the most obvious solution is better education (e.g., workshops, more working contacts) to erase false stereotypes and increase mutual understanding—if culture really is the major cause of faculty-administration adversity.

Newton's (2010) second explanation is that the causes often are more complex, arising from two different and incompatible models present in university settings. The *corporate model* is the one represented in the organizational chart and in the institutional charter. This model depicts governance by the board of trustees, to whom the president reports. In hierarchical order, under the president are the provost or senior vice president, then the deans of the schools. Department chairs, as the most junior members of the administration, report to deans. Faculty, not part of the administration, are located at the bottom of the chart, under the department chairs. Decisions come from the top by administrators obligated to stewardship. Whereas administrators are analogous to a firm's management, faculty members are viewed as employees without decision-making responsibility for the institution. They do not participate in setting policies or making major decisions because "their job is to teach." Administrators enforce this dichotomy by deliberately informing any vocal faculty that they are out of line.

However, faculty members may have difficulty reconciling themselves to be merely employees in a corporate organization. They consider themselves to be intelligent professionals who are affected by the administration's decisions collectively, personally, and in terms of their perceived ability to meet their callings. Without a fully participatory role, faculty sometimes resent those who do rule, manage, and administer. Faculty members' mistrust and opposition intensify when they perceive that the administration acts in ways contrary to their financial welfare or overall capacity to teach most effectively. This adversarial relationship can lead faculty to organize into a union. Although such collective action may be less likely in a Christian university because administrators can seek to counter it by appealing to their faculty's Christian commitment, distrust can remain.

According to Newton (2010), faculty members tend to prefer another explanatory model of the university, one that she designates the *college model*. Power emanates from the center of the organization, the locus of *truth* or *light*. This light attracts scholars who read, talk, think about the truth, and make it possible for others to understand it as well. The moral core of the university is a duty to pursue, preserve, and transmit faithfully the truth to those who gather around the scholars. (The motto of Oxford University is *God, enlighten me*.) Christian faculty might Platonically consider their focus on integrating faith and learning for Christian scholars as less tainted than the more worldly financial focus of the administration. However, since even scholars realize they have to make a living, they recognize their need for students. Faculty thus depend upon a supporting administrative apparatus to recruit, keep records, house and feed the students, and deal with other mundane administrative functions. Whereas the faculty views itself collectively as the employer and the administrators as necessary employees, faculty members find that they have little time or capability and less interest in governing the administrators. Thus, the faculty grows more and more dependent upon those they are supposed to be able to control, but cannot.

Conversely, on some college campuses the notion of shared governance can swing too far in the other direction. In extreme cases, certain faculty members can convince their colleagues to follow their lead in presenting powerful, negative roadblocks to the administrators' desired actions. When faculty effectively bully administrators into acting only in "their way," the board, president, and deans may not feel able to make difficult decisions for the good of the institution. The unfortunate result is that the president and deans can come to believe "we have the toughest roles on campus since we are the only ones who can lose our jobs because people can turn on us." Even the possibility of such a negative scenario suggests the need for the board, administration, and faculty to seek a collegial process, one that establishes a well-understood balance of power and responsibility that is appropriate for the pursuit of the institutional mission.

The bottom line is that the corporate and college models are fundamentally incompatible. Moreover, in their pure form, neither one seems adequate for ensuring the survival, much less the flourishing, of the university. Financial pressures, and the need for accountability to alumni and external bodies such as accrediting agencies, can be pressing. Some joint organizational approach, preferably a mutually agreeable one, is required. Can the models be integrated in a way that minimizes their respective weaknesses?

Newton (2010) answers by offering the *hospital* model of the university as a possible exemplar, wherein the medical doctors are compared to faculty and hospital administration is compared to university administration. In this model, the physicians focus on practicing health care and administrators watch expenses, the law, the regulators, and the public at large. Conflict is not eliminated, but it can be minimized if neither physicians nor administrators dominate. This requires both to understand that any ultimate winner will survive a power struggle with nothing more than a pyrrhic victory,

More critical than choosing any theoretical model for analyzing the culture is for the administration and the faculty to understand and respect one another. Even if both sides reach agreement on a consensual decision-making apparatus, the organization must also be structured to provide conflict management and mutual education. Systems thinking is recommended for this. Members of both faculty and administration need strength of will and proper humility to achieve cultural unity, consensually accepting the challenge of shaping and honing a culture of ethical integrity.

The cases that follow raise specific issues that administrators and faculty members are likely to face. Administrators might answer some of the case questions differently from the faculty discussants. Indeed, some of the issues might be considered more complex and relevant to faculty than they are to administrators. In actual practice, decision makers will need to interpret such ethical case situations and issues in light of their particular institution's culture and the history of its development. The preferred solutions are those that consider the possibility of differing value perspectives and the need to implement decisions with justice and love, with a dual leadership focus on improving the ethical culture for the future as well as simply making the one-off decisions for the situation at hand.

Leadership

The act of leading can be seen as a process that evolves and develops over time. Leadership can be studied as a science but must also be recognized as an art involving intangibles. Genuine leaders expect and are at home with ambiguity, paradox, and even contradiction (Banks & Ledbetter, 2004, p. 26).

Leadership is basically how persons move others to do something. "Defining *leadership* is simple: a leader is one who has followers," according to Christian businessman and consultant Fred Smith (1986). But developing a practical understanding of the *how* of leadership is a more difficult and more interesting challenge than merely defining it.

The really important leadership question is to define *good leadership* (Ciulla, 2004). Joanne Ciulla does this by specifying that a good leader is both ethical <u>and</u> effective. Scripture agrees. Psalm 78:72 honors David, whom God chose to be king: "So he shepherded them according to the integrity of his heart, and guided them with his skillful hands." Empirical research among American food industry managers also finds that followers most admire leaders who both live and lead according to a virtuous moral character and demonstrate competence in performing their organizational responsibilities. Moreover, they least admire those in whom they perceive character deficiencies (Whetstone, 2006).

When a person is appointed to a leadership position outside of his comfort area or above his level of competence, his new responsibilities, pressures, and opportunities may lead to ethical failures. Plato (1974) suggests this through his account of Socrates' dialogue on the moral failings of the fictional Gyges. This shepherd, after finding a magical ring that allowed him to be invisible, committed adultery with his queen, murdered his king, and married the widowed queen. His ring-enabled invisibility allowed Gyges to bypass normal societal constraints that previously prevented an ordinary shepherd and other citizens from even considering such crimes. Did his discovery and skillful use of the ring reveal his true inner immorality, or did it subvert the character that he previously manifested? Socrates did not reveal his own opinion. But the classic account of Gyges' ring suggests that leaders, including trustees and academic administrators, should strive to appoint only people of a sound moral character that complements their technical capacities. They should verify their choices via performance reviews tied to character assessment as well as numerical goals. They also are wise to demand the establishment and monitor the maintenance of an organizational culture that promotes virtue development and ethical practice (Whetstone, 2017).

The story of Gyges also suggests the significance of structural constraints. These should be made clear to all. For example, an institution's handbook should explicitly designate the decision-making responsibilities of administrators and faculty committees. All parties should understand what a committee is empowered to decide and whether that decision is binding or to be considered merely a recommendation to the campus leadership. Since effective decision-making and implementation requires that responsibility actually be equal to authority, if top administrators feel obligated to review and possibly reverse a committee decision, e.g., regarding a tenure decision that can result in a lawsuit, then the committee members will realize that they make recommendations rather than final decisions. This well may be appropriate because it can be difficult to hold a committee or even its chairperson responsible in such cases.

Administrators should not be tyrannical, but neither can the faculty behave like "inmates who run the asylum." As a specific example, faculty committee appointments can be balanced to elicit input from a wide representation of the faculty, not allowing the same individuals to dominate by serving on influential committees too often or too long. And because many faculty tend to be careful people, they sometimes hold their tongues while allowing a few strong voices to dominate a discussion. This is especially likely when tenured faculty serve alongside those who are not yet tenured. To encourage participation from all, committee and department chairpersons need to appreciate such structural hurdles and lead so as to overcome them.

Leadership Challenges of Faculty Administrators

Academic administrators face leadership challenges atypical to those of leaders of other types of organizations. These can arise due to the administration-faculty culture clashes previously discussed.

Those administrators appointed from faculty positions can approach their new roles with considerable awareness and insight, but they still must adapt to a new approach to thinking. This involves and requires a shift to an institutional perspective, a shift in the kinds of issues identified and addressed, and a shift in the kind of ethical reasoning required to address those issues. Brian Schrag (2010) describes from his own experience the shifts in ethical perspective when one moves from the role of a faculty member to that of an academic administrator. He explains that there is a shift from moral reasoning for purposes of judging, to that of moral reasoning for purposes of taking action. Faculty, as moral critics and judges, typically are not involved in solving practical administrative problems; rather, they make judgments of actions already taken. As a moral agent, an administrator needs to focus on practical judgment to guide action as opposed to retrospective judgments on actions already taken (Schrag, 2010, p. 28). This requires looking forward, often with only partial information, under a tight time constraint for making a decision. Moral reasoning can be messy (in terms of theoretical ethics) and the alternative chosen may involve compromise. Nevertheless, the administrator as moral agent still needs to preserve his integrity and that of his institution. The magnitude or extent of the shift to practical ethical reasoning (from the activity of critic and judge to the activity of choosing a course of action) increases as one moves up the administrative hierarchy, being least dramatic for department chairs and most pronounced for presidents.

It is especially critical that a new president appointed from a non-academic institutional background, such as the military or business, strive to understand the cognitive gap in practical ethical reasoning that can occur between faculty and administration. He needs to learn when to move from debate and analysis to decision implementation. And he must resist feeling personally attacked when faculty critique or question his directives as he gains experience and wisdom.

The need to compromise can be great in academia because of a culture clash between a top-down mentality of the administration and the consultative, participatory preference of faculty. Schrag (2010) views this as dysfunctional but suggests it can be improved by making faculty members more aware of both their need to cultivate an atmosphere of civility on campus and also their professional responsibilities to act as trustees of the educational program of their institution. Faculty must help create and maintain a culture that will sustain a community of learners. However, the administrators have responsibility to support these ideals as well. If only one of the groups honestly seeks resolution whereas the other does not, then the resulting power imbalance can lead to either institutional bankruptcy or faculty demoralization.

Lack of perceived attention to the spiritual mission of a Christian institution can be another serious cause of disunity. The ideal Christian college employs administrators, faculty, and staff who have a genuine sense of calling to serve Christ, and through Him, the mission and students. Because this is the heartfelt desire of many drawn to faculty and to administration, if they come to believe it is not being realized, serious frustration and feelings of being offended and manipulated can simmer and sometimes flare.

Administration leaders can ameliorate organizational tensions by exemplifying sound ethical practices. Others notice how leaders interpret and implement policies and whether they wisely allow exceptions in unusual situations. Consultation with a committee of faculty and/or students and other available resources, such as the university attorney or outside consultants, is often helpful. However, because they need to act in a timely manner, academic administrators make many decisions routinely without broad consultation (Loui, 2010, p. 136). Loui says he uses two ethical tests: the newspaper principle and his Kantian deontological test as to whether allowing a particular exception could be justified for adoption as part of the general policy. He advises the administrator to make a process more public, getting more—and the right—people involved. This and the discipline of following a formal collective process increase trust. Of course, the leader must responsibly balance needs for confidentiality with openness in the process.

It is incumbent on a higher level administrator to support the authority of subordinate administrators. For example, a dean should not allow a faculty member to bypass his department chair; the dean should refer the disgruntled faculty back to his chair or, when resolution of a conflict is appropriate at the higher level, be careful to investigate and hear the positions of all sides. Neither should a president or provost allow individual faculty members or committees to bypass the dean. Violation of the management principle of line of authority inevitably has costs that should not be overlooked.

For her overall leadership approach, a leader should consider the tradeoffs between a democratic, participatory decision-making approach and a hierarchical one. Whereas the former may result in greater consensus, the latter can be more efficient. A leader might well review the account of Jethro's advice to Moses (Exod. 19) and other scripture passages (e.g., Matt. 18 and 2 Tim. 2:14-26) as he seeks to adapt to his particular leadership strengths, the capabilities of his faculty, and the institutional culture.

Administrators can become frustrated when their directives are resisted. Faculty department chairs often face difficult challenges with their faculty in implementing policy changes considered straightforward by their administrators. This phenomenon is attributable to a unique feature of the typical university structure. Chairpersons are caught in the middle between the expectations of their department's faculty and those of deans and other administrators (Pritchard, 2010). Administrators tend to view faculty chairs as part of management, appointed by the deans and serving at their discretion. Chairs are thus expected to intervene when individual faculty members violate norms.

But positive leadership is required to persuade faculty members to go beyond their primary focus on their specific teaching and research commitments (and the responsibility of building a collegial faculty team) to think and question how they can assess the appropriateness of programs in terms of institutional mission and the long-term best interests of the institution (Schrag, 2010). Pritchard and Schrag, after assuming administrative roles, found the vision of faculty to be rather narrow; the administrator needs to move them from a primary orientation on "my problems" to one addressing "our (e.g., our institution's) problems."

For example, when preparing budget submissions, the chair needs to win, and certainly not lose, in the eyes of his faculty in the competition with other departments for funds (Pritchard, 2010). When other departments routinely "pad" their submissions as a buffer against cuts to be applied proportionately to submissions, should the department chair join in the padding or should he refuse to play this ethically questionable game? If he submits the reasonable amounts he feels his department needs and is awarded less, he might remain true to his personal ethic, but also disappoint his faculty, even losing their trust and respect. Of course, the school's budget administrator should seek to prevent budget padding, but his efforts can fall short in the typical political and competitive administrative environment.

Systematic and situational difficulties can confront university administrators at each level. Good leaders recognize and strive to overcome such social challenges as they build an ethical culture focused on fulfilling the institutional mission.

The Virtues of an Academic Administrator

Technical skills are necessary but insufficient for a good leader. Even more important is the leader's moral character. What personal virtues does a university administrator most need if she is to help move the institution toward its mission ethically within the culture of the organization? Taking an Aristotelian approach, Curren (2010) proposes three key characteristics: commitment to the good of the institution, good administrative judgment, and conscientiousness in discharging the duties of the office, elements he describes as cardinal virtues for academic administration. The first virtue is teleological: the academic administrator must act with a commitment to the well-being or good of the institution (Curren, 2010, p. 64). Further, having accepted the duties of an administrative office, a person is ethically obligated to fulfill them conscientiously for the duration of her appointment. And, for decision-making and implementation, one's deontological commitment to conscientiousness calls upon wise moral judgment or *phronesis*, which Aristotle classifies as an intellectual virtue that presupposes all the moral virtues since it is essential to any of them being a true virtue. Indeed, Beabout (2012) argues that practical wisdom (Aristotle's *phronesis* or Aquinas' *prudentia*) is the highest and most essential virtue enabling pursuit of the common good in the business organization. In like fashion, Curren (2010) designates practical wisdom as a distinct ethically laden virtue of academic administration because it is so central to good leadership.

Curren further argues that the essential elements of leader character can be captured in the concept of *integrity*. This includes both the notions of rectitude, or the sum of honesty, fairness, and other such traits, and of being true to oneself, being faithful to a consistent set of important commitments. Moreover, a person of integrity must be beyond just being true to self. Integrity in the academic administrator entails not only personal integrity, the form associated with common morality and applicable in everyday life, but also having a disposition to act with integrity in fulfilling one's duties (McFall, 2003, p. 69).

A Christian in university administration can also appeal to spiritual help through diligent application of Christian virtues. These include faith, hope, and love (1 Cor. 13) as well as knowledge, self-control, perseverance, godliness, and brotherly kindness (2 Pet. 1:5-7). He can call upon the fruits of the Spirit (Gal. 5:22-23) even as he labors on what some call the dark side, applying them with humility, without boastfulness or envy (Gal. 5:26). Proper humility is neither soft nor weak; instead it requires honestly recognizing and applying abilities courageously toward the welfare of the institution and its constituents. A properly humble academic administrator takes responsibility for his team's failures and recognizes others for its successes. Indeed, a biblical worldview supports Jim Collins's (2001) empirically grounded common grace insight that the best (Level 5) business leaders are genuinely and personally humble while aggressively committed to the success of their organizations.

Perhaps the most distinctive outworking of a Christian's leadership ethic is his ability and willingness to forgive. He can exercise forgiveness to repentant students, colleagues, and other constituents, balancing this with his commitment to justice and fairness. He should demonstrate that he allows others to make a mistake, and he should admit and seek to correct his own mistakes. This attitude not only helps maintain trust but also allows for more innovation in pursuit of the mission.

A Christian should understand forgiveness because God has forgiven him. God also commands him to forgive others. Whereas repentance and forgiveness are not magic elixirs for organizational health, they can help promote a culture that seeks to identify and implement policies, procedures, and other structural means for enhancing trust. These benefits improve the practice of ethical leadership, a process that is positive when people, starting with the leader, grow more sanctified in their moral character and behaviors.

A Christian university or college administrator is a person called by God, first as a Christian and also as a leader. To be a good leader, she must learn to grow in effectiveness as a technically competent leader. A leader who is a Christian also needs to develop and grow in her cognitive, moral, and emotional commitment to a biblical worldview as she develops those virtues needed for applying a sound Christian ethic.

Being willing to act in faith, the leader in a Christian institution needs to identify with its mission as worthy and achievable. If he sincerely does, he can strive to convince others of this and to exemplify through his relationships and behaviors a commitment to operate consistently and cooperatively toward achieving the mission. He must mold and personally exemplify the cultural values of the institution and strive to assure that his followers are rightly fitted to their responsibilities and have the supportive organizational structure, resources, and motivation to join with him for successful fulfillment of the mission to the glory of God.

Chapter Three presents a model for ethical decision-making. It provides an overall guide for sound ethical analysis and the discussion of the cases that follow.

Chapter Three

A Model for Ethical Decision-making

New and troubling situations often confront administrators. They are expected to accept the responsibility for deciding how best to address potential problems in an ethical manner. A good leader desires to make a wise move, but the best solution initially may not be obvious. And if the situation has unique features involving relationships among diverse personalities, it can demand prompt attention to ameliorate boiling tensions that can grow quickly into major problems. Moreover, while promoting an essential need for ethical leadership, President Kerry D. Romesburg of Jacksonville University admits, "Too often it is difficult, if not impossible, to apply an overriding ethical system to individual situations and circumstances" (2010, p. 10).

A leader's decisions can be misunderstood and mistakes are not unlikely, especially when decision time is short and information is imperfect. Nevertheless, the administrator should not fear to appeal to her common sense understanding of right and wrong, while avoiding making knee-jerk responses before understanding the differing points of view. Others are watching and will assess her based on how they perceive she acts, whether she sought to make a wise and just choice concerning the particular situation.

Although all this can be challenging, growing as an ethical decision maker is an essential part of being a good administrator, one who brings creativity to her ethical analysis, as well as a growing understanding of situations and contexts, the organizational culture, and organizational members and their relationships. Reliance on taking a pragmatic approach is insufficient for this; even the most assured administrators must resist acceptance of pragmatic relativism as their most realistic fallback position. Instead, as Bernard Gert explains, "Although there is not always one morally acceptable way of acting, in every moral situation there are morally better and morally worse ways of acting" (2004). Even though a person can choose mistakenly or implement decisions poorly, over time she can seek to learn and implement corrective measures, thereby molding a more ethical culture. Her workplace and life experiences moreover can help her grow in moral wisdom, in correctly discerning right from wrong.

Education in basic ethics theories and organizational decision-making approaches is most advisable. This chapter presents a straightforward model of principled, ethical decision-making and a brief introduction of some major ethics theories to which a thoughtful person can refer when tackling the cases that follow. Readers schooled in ethics might choose to skip this chapter and go immediately to some of the cases that follow. Others might benefit from considering the model and theoretical principles and seek to apply them to the case questions. Each reader should be able to benefit from further investigation in the field of ethics. This, combined with thoughtful review of her own experiences, will help the committed administrator to develop and hone her personal guidelines for ethical analysis and thus ethical leadership.

The suggested process for approaching ethical decision-making is outlined in Exhibit 1. It differs from traditional management decision models that start with problem definition (e.g., see Garvin, 1993), instead beginning with recognition that the most basic ethical problem is not always clear at the outset. This is especially the case when an individual brings a complaint about another, requesting corrective action. When a student or faculty member brings his concerns, a wise university administrator first investigates by consulting the other party and possibly seeking additional sources of information to understand better what the problem really is. Then begins the process of problem definition, generation of alternative solutions, comparative assessment of reasonable alternatives, and selection of the most appropriate one or the wisest combination of the alternatives. Acting to implement the decision is critical and thus requires careful consideration. As in all leadership models, the final step is monitoring results and following up as needed.

Exhibit 1 also differs from the more traditional rational model offered for academic administrators by Englehardt (2010, p. xxiv) because it draws on a biblical worldview. In particular, it elaborates the follow-up phase, emphasizing the importance of forgiveness followed by attention to an ethical growth process, analogous to spiritual sanctification, that seeks to improve organizational structures and policies so as to inhibit reoccurrences of the ethical problems. It thus highlights the importance of ethical improvement over time rather than exclusive focus on a one-off decision.

Ethical Criteria

Ethical analysis is not always difficult. Actually acting ethically, implementing an ethical solution, often is harder—and more important—than determining what the ethical choice should be. But thoughtful analysis is nevertheless essential. As a start, the administrator can apply heuristics or rules-of-thumb such as the Golden Rule, the newspaper principle (would he be comfortable seeing his decision reported in the newspaper), or the Ethics Check (Blanchard & Peale, 1988). In the latter, the decision maker answers three questions in sequential order. First, is the considered action a legal one? If so, is it balanced or most fair to all parties affected (the stakeholders)? If reasonably balanced, will the act not offend the decision maker's conscience? According to the Ethics Check, if all three questions can be answered positively, then the decision maker may proceed with the action.

While simple heuristics are often helpful, some situations can require more in-depth analysis. For example, consider the Ethics Check. Following the letter of the law is not always the same as being ethical. Moreover, balancing anticipated consequences can be subjective, and one's conscience is not always a good guide, for it can be hardened and seared. Puritan Richard Sibbes (1862) noted that his conscience was his best friend but also his greatest enemy.

Following the decision steps of Exhibit 1 leads to a more rigorous analysis, one informed by a philosophical approach consistent with Christian theology. Applying it calls for thoughtful attention to each step in the process, including problem definition, alternative generation, and the plan for implementation as well as analysis of available alternatives. These steps are interrelated and thus not always followed in strict linear sequence. Throughout the process, the decision maker generally draws on ethics theories, which place primary focus on either (1) the anticipated results or consequences of an act (outcomes), (2) the means used in acting (rights, justice), or (3) the moral character of the person acting (virtue). Exhibit 2 briefly describes these basic ethics theories.

Since the various ethics theories sometimes point to differing choices, which one should the decision maker use? Sison (2006), Whetstone (2001, 2003, 2006), and others have suggested combining the three major philosophical ethical frameworks within a complementary tripartite ethic. This approach seeks to acknowledge the focus of each

Exhibit 1

Steps for Ethical Decision-making

1. **Get the facts**

2. **Define the problem or ethical issues**

3. **Generate alternative solutions**

4. **Evaluate the alternatives**

   —Identify all affected stakeholders

   —Anticipate consequences for each stakeholder group

   —Apply ethical decision criteria

   -consequential utilitarianism—costs & benefits

   -rights & justice—duties, obligations, principles

   -character or virtue ethics

5. **Choose the preferred solution**

6. **Implement the solution**

7. **Follow up**

   —Monitor to evaluate results

   —Correct

   —Forgive

   —Grow

theory in turn. The decision maker analyzes an alternative decision in terms of each of the three ethics theories: its anticipated consequences (ends) for all stakeholders, concerns as to rights and justice (means applied), and the moral character dispositions (virtues and vices) of the person acting. Often the criteria will point to the same choice, strengthening its justification. If the criteria point to different choices, the decision maker will have to draw on his experienced judgment (practical wisdom) to select the ethical focus that best applies to the case at hand. He then will choose his preferred alternative solution, or perhaps decide to combine aspects of two or more alternatives to reach a superior choice.

For an example, consider the following case. A dean must decide whether or not to propose a new program that he suspects will initially be opposed by some of the other schools within the university. He has funds in his budget for hiring a consultant who can design and help sell the program. Should he hire the consultant and proceed? Utilitarian calculations of anticipated consequences might support this decision in terms of the net additional revenues that can be projected for the university versus the opportunity costs of not proceeding with other alternatives. But do any institutional policies provide roadblocks? If not, and he does proceed, he should monitor the consultant's activities and assure that the rights of all affected parties are protected. As discussed in chapter two, the dean also must weigh his decision in light of the institutional mission. And a wise administrator will not just check off each option but consider them in light of likely impacts on the important relationships in the organizational culture. Further, will the contemplated action and the means for implementing it not only promote his image, but more importantly, be characteristic of the sort of leader he wishes to be in terms of his sense of Christian calling and personal moral character? If his answers to these questions point in the same direction, the decision should be straightforward. However, if the results are mixed, then the leader is called upon to exercise his practical judgment (*phronesis*) to weigh the relative importance of the differing criteria for the decision at hand. For the Christian, prayer for God's wisdom should permeate the entire decision process.

Scripture supports such a tripartite formulation for a comprehensive Christian ethic. God, through Moses, reiterated the people's obligation to obey the Moral Law (means, duties), which requires a righteous heart within them (character virtue), in order to achieve God's intended purpose and consequences for them (Dt. 4:29). Micah 6:8 refers to justice as God's purpose, kindness as the means (rule for right behavior), and humility as a characteristic virtue of the actor. Jesus used the image of the heart, and Paul wrote several lists of virtues forming the nature of the righteous heart. Note that Paul describes walking by the Spirit as being humble (not boastful, challenging one another, envying one another) (Gal. 5:26), which is the proper attitude for practicing the fruit of the Spirit (Gal. 5:22-23). The heart is the internal moral character needed to behave according to the Moral Law. A tripartite Christian ethic is graciously empowered by the Holy Spirit throughout; it requires the faith that comes from spiritual regeneration and involves spiritual development of the person's moral character, through sanctification, to obey the Moral Law in seeking God's will (see Phil. 2:12-13).

Exhibit 2

A Brief Comparison of Ethics Theories

After getting the facts that apply to an ethical problem situation, criteria are needed to assess relevant policies, institutions, and behaviors (not judging people themselves) and to reach an appropriate decision. There are three basic types of ethics principles: consequentialism, rights, and justice.

Probably the most commonly applied consequentialist principle for decision-making is that of utility. One chooses the action or behavior that is expected to produce the greatest good for the greatest number. The ultimate criterion is consequentialist, based on expected results or outcomes (quantification of benefits less costs) to all the stakeholders affected by an action.

Another principle, that of rights, is not primarily concerned with maximizing quantitative outcomes but serves to protect the rights and freedom of people impacted by an act. A right can be positive, such as the right to meaningful employment or education, or negative, such as the rights not to be murdered, robbed of property, or sexually harassed. People differ as to what they believe rights are, especially regarding positive rights. People also do not always recognize the responsibilities that accompany rights. If one has a right not to be sexually harassed on the job, then not only must employees not harass others, but the organization's leadership has a responsibility to maintain a workplace structure and culture that minimizes the opportunity for harassment and that effectively disciplines those who engage in harassing behavior.

The principle of justice also focuses on responsibilities or obligations; it, like rights, is thus called deontological (referring to duties). Justice is a very thick concept, having many levels of meaning and interpretations. Most basically, justice relates to how equitably or fairly the benefits and the burdens or costs of an action are shared between people, or among the members of a group, organization, or society. Some see justice requiring equality of outcomes, whereas others, especially social conservatives and classical liberals, stress the need for equality of opportunity, a level playing field, although this will allow some to achieve more and thus receive more than others.

Note that, while utilitarianism focuses on ends, consequences, or results, rights and justice put greater priority on duties and obligations, means over ends.

All three approaches consider both ends or consequences and means. These approaches are impersonal in not relating to the personal character of the actor or the nature of people affected. Utilitarianism, rights, and justice each can be interpreted and applied in differing ways. Philosophers continue to debate them and their relative importance.

But what if the approaches point to conflicting decisions and acts? For example, utilitarians as consequentialists in some situations calculate a positive value for misrepresenting the truth—spinning or lying. In a dictatorship, should one lie to the police who are seeking to find a political opponent (e.g., a Jew in Nazi Germany) who is hiding in the house? Should the person tell the police that the Jew is not there in order to protect him from unjust persecution or even a death camp? Before answering yes, she should remember that God's Law teaches that lying is a sin. Most ethical decisions are not so difficult or dramatic, but one still needs good judgment, including a large dose of common sense, to decide what decision is most ethical when considerations of consequences, rights, and justice conflict, pointing to different answers.

A decision justified by utilitarian logic also can be unjust; producing the greatest good or utility for the greatest number or majority can cause a minority to suffer injustice. A tragic example from

American history was pointed out to this writer when he taught courses in Cherokee, North Carolina. After hearing about the principles of utility and justice, one young Cherokee woman commented, "Oh, you mean it was like what happened to us?" In the 1830s, the Cherokee and other tribes (actually nations) who had treaties with the United States were forcibly removed from their lands to Oklahoma. Many lost all their land and most of their possessions and large numbers died along the Trail of Tears due to cruel treatment and the incompetence of those transporting them. From a purely utilitarian perspective, however, this was a good outcome because the American population was able to grow westward, creating the great nation of today. The greatest number certainly benefited; it can even be argued that the Cherokee people of today as citizens share in the resulting benefits. However, was stealing land from civilized, largely Christian tribes that had legal treaties guaranteeing their land rights, and forcing the people on a long march involving starvation, disease, and great suffering, at all just? Utility maximization can result in grave injustice.

So which ethical principle is best? When should one apply utility or rights or justice to make the decision that is the most ethical? All three are important and can lead to ethical decisions. Sometimes none of them offers a completely satisfactory answer, especially to the most difficult ethical questions. A recommended approach is to consider an ethical situation or case from all three perspectives, weighing the utilitarian benefits and costs expected from a particular decision, while guarding the rights of each major stakeholder group impacted, and seeking the most just balance or fairness to all. One considers both ends and means.

Actually making the best decision requires strong character. Yet another theoretical ethics perspective, virtue ethics, is more concerned about the moral qualities and integrity of the person facing an ethical decision than it is in the specific decision to act. "Are you acting as the person you want to be?" is a more central question for virtue ethics than, "Did you make the right decision in terms of consequences and means?" Gary Weaver (2017, p. 614) says that virtue ethics emphasizes experience and relationships for virtue development whereas emphasis on decision criteria, formal training and cognitive development forms much of organizational and policy efforts to foster ethical behavior in business. Virtue ethics is concerned with what it means to be a person of moral integrity and how one can grow in moral character. Rather than competing with the other theories, it should complement the principles of utility, rights, and justice through its emphasis on why a person is inclined (even motivated) to do (not just know) what is right and just and good to do, even when this involves significant personal sacrifice. Readers can find an example of a practical virtue ethics leadership approach in Kouzes and Posner's *Credibility* (2003) and Whetstone's *Leadership Ethics & Spirituality* (2013, 2019).

Using the Decision Model

Theoretically, a rational model assumes perfect information, the ability to identify and rank all solution alternatives using objective criteria, and the existence of an optimal solution that will provide maximum benefits to the organization and all parties concerned. These ideal requirements can be rigorous or impossible to achieve. Therefore, experienced decision makers rarely follow a traditional decision model in mechanical, lock-step fashion, objecting that doing so is not always practical. They know that tough choices may have to be made quickly in dynamic, complex environments. It can be difficult to find all relevant information and completely analyze all possible alternatives, given normal limitations on time and research resources.

In practice, some decision makers use other approaches. March and Simon (1993) have famously said that individuals tend rather to satisfice, to use a bounded rationality model in day-to-day decision-making. People tend to choose the most satisfactory alternative that will address the problem in a theoretically imperfect, but workable, fashion (March & Simon, 1993; March, 1994). Instead of insisting on the perfect solution, they apply rational reason to choose the more acceptable decision after a limited search for alternatives. The most acceptable alternative might be the one that is easiest to identify and achieve, least controversial, or safer than the one that is theoretically optimal. The satisficing approach is imperfect but superior to others sometimes used, such as the political model. For the latter, an administrator defers to the distribution of power within the organization, ultimately for her own self-interests. The political model is particularly apt for a postmodern worldview, although it is problematic for Christians. Admittedly, on some occasions the solution that ultimately proves best is actually stumbled upon through serendipity.

The ethics decision-making model of Exhibit 1 nevertheless outlines a reasonable approach for analyzing the cases in this book; it highlights the analytical components and ethical criteria that deserve consideration. A sound reasoning process is important because it leads to decision-making empowerment (better decisions that one can better justify) and guidance for implementing and explaining one's ethical actions.

In actual practice, the sophisticated decision maker might adapt the theoretical ethics decision-making model in several ways. The numbered steps need not always be completed in the same sequence. The administrative leader facing a problem often cannot wait for all the facts or even know all relevant information at the outset. Even when analyzing a written case, a person might need to read and reread the case to filter out the irrelevant details from the most pertinent ones before generating and choosing alternative solutions. In the workplace, data gathering should undergird all process steps. Indeed, openness to new information should continue throughout the process, sometimes resulting in a revision of alternatives or even a redefinition of the problem. This usually calls for observation and active research and a commitment to weigh all pertinent facts and opinions in light of the environmental context and history of the organization's personalities and relationships, cultural values, and mission (see chapter two), as well as the financial, technological, and other factors potentially affecting the problem. Creative thinking or moral imagination (Werhane, 1999) is required for thorough analysis. As he applies ethical criteria, the administrator as leader needs to consider the interests and responsibilities of all stakeholders in a decision, any mitigating circumstances, and his ability to act. In addition, a spiritually-minded leader will appeal to prayer and often to wise counsel as he actually proceeds toward a decision. In the end, due to the pressures of time and limited resources, he might have to choose the most satisfactory option and move forward.

Even more important than making the best, most ethically defensible, one-off human decision is the attempt to make changes in policies, procedures, structural relationships, or even personnel assignments to mitigate the likelihood of future recurrences of the problem. The administrator must realistically expect some imperfect outcomes, but can still attain a measure of successful ethical leadership if he and the organization profit from their experience, thereby learning how to improve the ethical culture and reduce the future frequency of ethical shortcomings. This is why the manner of implementation and subsequent follow-up are critical. Effective follow-up requires evaluation of results, implementation of corrective measures, and often forgiveness. Sincere follow-up effort can lead to ethical growth in the parties involved and in the administrator. As discussed in chapter two, forgiveness is an advantage Christians have and should employ in ethical decision-making.

Final Thoughts for Academic Administrators

Werner (2010) identifies three spheres as being especially important for academic administration professionals (Badaracco, 1995). These are personal values and ethics, professional ethical obligations, and leadership responsibilities. An administrator must balance these sometimes competing spheres when making decisions. Effective academic leaders not only seek to involve faculty in planning and decision-making to build a culture of respect, trust, and collaboration, but, to seek creative solutions, they also invite debate, even dissension, on issues (Berenbeim, 2007). In this, all those involved should acknowledge that neither professional obligations nor leadership responsibilities replace or overshadow one's personal values and ethics.

Decision-making leaders should also note with caution what Alexis de Tocqueville (1969) wrote on Kant's reference to "the radical evil"— using the language of ethics as a screen or tool for self-love and self-interest (Aeschliman, 2007). A person can slip into this habit almost without noticing. A Christian should guard against flippant use of "church language" and avoid attributing her personal willful desires to the leading of the Holy Spirit. She should question whether a desire, even one supporting what she feels is a good overall purpose, is really justified ethically and biblically. She should apply sound ethical analysis to justify and prepare to explain decisions to avoid falling into "the radical evil" temptation.

Apparent ethical quandaries often arise from the tensions between personal values, professional obligations, and leadership role responsibilities. The cases that follow involve some of the diverse situations and issues that university administrators and faculty face due to such tensions. Analysis and discussion of the cases can provide a laboratory for addressing those ethical challenges that they will inevitably face.

Additional helpful resources also are available. The Association for Professional and Practical Ethics (www.indiana.edu/~appe/) and The Society for Ethics Across the Curriculum (www.rit.edu/~6929www/seac/) have recently started to address ethics issues in academic administration.

Chapter Four

Cases Involving the President and the Staff and Faculty

The following cases depict situations and decisions in Christian colleges and universities. The names used for individuals and institutions are purely fictional. The objective is to stimulate thought rather than to criticize any particular person or organization. Such cases can help concerned Christians seriously ponder their administrative practices and attitudes and provide a basis for further discussion. It is hoped this will result in the clarification of what a contemporary university administration ethic might be, a *via affirmativa*, when empowered by the grace of the Lord Jesus Christ under the true and perfect inspiration of the Holy Spirit.

This collection organizes the cases according to the university rank of the primary decision maker. In chapter four this is the president of the institution, especially in Case 1 "Choice of an Executive Assistant" and Case 2 "The President Meets the Faculty." People at other levels are obviously also involved and may well face similar decision-making situations. Case 3 "Hitting the Wall" describes an unpleasant experience that can personally affect faculty and administrators of any level.

The provost or academic dean is a key protagonist in the cases of chapter five, especially in her professional relationships with department chairs and other faculty. Case 4 "Full-time Adjuncts," Case 5 "Termination of a Christian Employee," Case 6 "The In-group of True Believers," and Case 7 "An Open Door Policy" feature only a small sampling of the wide variety of issues, great and small, faculty raise to their provosts and academic deans for decisions.

As written, the cases of chapter six: Case 8 "Investigation of MBA Programs" and Case 9 "The Special Lady," present faculty department chairs in the primary decision-making role. Higher administrators and other faculty can expect to face similar issues at their levels.

Chapter seven includes two cases on the unpleasant subject of contested student grades. Case 10 is "The Threatening Father" and Case 11 is "The Aspiring Academic All-American." The course instructor and department chair are most immediately involved, but special cases such as these can and do sometimes bring in the president as well as deans.

Case 12 "The Consultant Who Felt Bilked" is the sole case in chapter eight. A dean and a faculty chair are the key actors in this case write-up. But since it also involves contractual relationships with an outside party, it merely represents a variety of issues that require institutional policies because of potential legal and public relations impacts.

Questions are listed after each case to help initiate and guide discussion. After Case 1 "The Choice of an Executive Assistant" (Whetstone, 2005a) readers will find a discussion of possible answers to each question based on previously unpublished teaching notes that have been successfully used in undergraduate class discussions.

CASE 1: Choice of an Executive Assistant

Jack Brown, an active member of his local church, genuinely desires to serve as a Christian leader. At the age of 42, he was recently hired as the president of ZYX College. The previous president's executive assistant, Miss Emma Cummings, who has served thirty years as personal secretary/executive assistant to the last six presidents, decided that it is a good time for her to retire. This will allow Mr. Brown to appoint her successor as he begins his responsibilities.

The executive assistant to the president serves a strategic role. Whereas the top officers generally have only a few years' tenure, especially in any one position, the executive assistants often make a career of their roles, having proven their institutional loyalty, skill, and intelligence by moving up from other secretarial positions in the organization. They do not make policy decisions but are most influential regarding access to policy makers. They value the public reputation and integrity of the college and are gatekeepers between the president and its stakeholders, including owners, trustees, administrators, staff, faculty, students, and the public-at-large.

The Human Resources Department, after screening the pool of applicants, sends three to President Brown for interviews. Each meets the technical and legal requirements for the position of executive assistant. Unless he wants to restart the entire search process, President Brown must select one of the following:

> Cynthia Whyte, 30, a college-educated teacher with excellent computer skills. Two years ago she married the Vice President, Finance of ZYX College. They have had no children and she says she wishes to assume a full-time position for her personal career development. She emphasizes that she already knows the college well because of her husband.

<u>Edgar Greene</u>, 33, an employee of ZYX's Advancement Office. Since joining the staff three years ago, he has received outstanding performance reviews and has a track record of productive suggestions. He has completed two years of college and is unmarried. He says that he is seeking the position as a way to broaden his experience.

<u>Amanda Blue</u>, 56, a widow, is a recent early retiree who served 20 years as an executive assistant in ABC College, a Christian school in another state. She says that she seeks the executive assistant position because she misses her work, having realized she is a long way from needing to retire. In addition, whereas she recently moved to the community in order to be close to her grandchildren, she now realizes that she should work so as not to interfere too much with the child-raising efforts of her son and daughter-in-law.

After interviewing each of the candidates, Jack Brown is convinced that each is well qualified in terms of the technical skills listed in the job specifications and that each, based on reference checks and interview discussions, appears to be a person of good Christian character. Moreover, each candidate appears to understand the requirements in the formal job description and has confirmed that he or she will accept the job, if offered. Jack faces a difficult choice and wants to do so with godly wisdom.

Jack wonders if he needs to consider anything else, any special circumstances or relationship factors that will help him to determine the most appropriate choice. He wonders whether it would be culturally appropriate to hire a male as his personal executive assistant. He is unsure how he would relate to a significantly older personal assistant. He and his wife already have a close acquaintance with Cynthia, not only because of college gatherings but also because they attend the same church, belonging to the same neighborhood ministry group. Edgar Greene and Amanda Blue regularly attend other churches whose pastors have supplied good character references.

Jack has been very impressed with Bernard Whyte as a capable and innovative financial executive, one who is enthusiastic about some major changes President Brown thinks ZYX College needs to meet its strategic objectives. In particular, Bernard has proposed hiring a small computer consulting firm with expertise in college administration. Jack knows this firm founded by Bernard's uncle very well, having worked with it while at other colleges. Jack sees Bernard Whyte as someone with whom he needs to work closely in building the college, but wonders whether the faculty and staff members would see his hiring of Bernard's wife in the strategic gatekeeper role of executive assistant as an appropriate choice.

Author's note: This case is closely based upon one previously published in Whetstone, J. T. (2005). *Journal of Biblical Integration and Business, Special Issue: Cases with a Christian Worldview*. Christian Business Faculty Association, pp. 65-67. The only significant revision is the change of Jack Brown's position to that of President of ZYX College rather than ZYX Corporation. The discussion in response to the case questions is previously unpublished.

QUESTIONS:

1. Before deciding to whom he should first offer the executive assistant position, Jack Brown reviews what he understands are the responsibilities of a Christian leader. What are some of the relevant requirements that Jack might consider in his hiring decision? What potential problems should he seek to avoid?

2. The Bible teaches the wisdom of seeking counsel (Proverbs 15:22). Should Jack do so in this case? In particular, should he consult with Miss Emma Cummings?

3. Which of the three candidates, if anyone, should Jack be most reluctant to hire as his next executive assistant? Explain.

4. Which of the three candidates should Jack select?

DISCUSSION OF CASE 1: ONE SET OF ANSWERS:

1. Before addressing the issue of whom President Jack Brown should hire, the instructor might lead a discussion of the distinctives of a Christian approach to leadership. This can emphasize the spiritual nature and importance of the selection decision. Additional considerations are suggested below.

    Although the Bible is not a leadership textbook, and Christ did not teach leadership by formal declarations, he did demonstrate servant leadership by his personal example (e.g., Is. 53; John 13). Christ's basic organizing principle is servant leadership (Sanders, 1980). Jack Brown would be wise to consider how this applies to his executive role.

    To focus the discussion, the instructor also could refer to sources such as Chewning, Eby, and Roels' *Business Through the Eyes of Faith* (1990). They offer a most helpful discussion of godly leadership, listing the following responsibilities of a Christian leader:

    > Christian leaders are models of moral behavior, and often a tougher standard is applied to Christians than is applied to others. Leaders are responsible to articulate and carry out the vision for the organization. Leaders are responsible to maintain open communication—clear, simple, unambiguous, and to the point. Christian leaders are responsible for team building, based on a high level of trust. Christian leaders are responsible to create environments that encourage and facilitate growth and creativity. Leaders must also manage the functions and procedures of an organization. (pp.137-140)

Although he is writing specifically about the requirements for church officers, Paul's advice to Timothy applies to the case at hand.

> This is a true saying, If a man desire the office of a bishop, he desireth a good work. A bishop then must be blameless, the husband of one wife, vigilant, sober, of good behaviour, given to hospitality, apt to teach; Not given to wine, no striker, not greedy of filthy lucre; but patient, not a brawler, not covetous; One that ruleth well his own house, having his children in subjection with all gravity; (For if a man know not how to rule his own house, how shall he take care of the church of God?) Not a novice, lest being lifted up with pride he fall into the condemnation of the devil. Moreover, he must have a good report of them which are without; lest he fall into reproach and the snare of the devil. (1 Tim. 3:1-7)

Discussants might identify which of the requirements and responsibilities apply most directly to President Brown's current hiring decision. Reputation and the perceptions of others matter. Jack should be especially concerned about how his decision will be perceived by those he is responsible for leading. He should take great care to follow the admonition of James 3:17, "But the wisdom that is from above is first pure, then peaceable, gentle, and easy to be intreated, full of mercy and good fruits, without partiality, and without hypocrisy." He should avoid the appearance of hiring anyone who could even be perceived as having a conflict of interest.

2. A long-serving executive assistant, such as Miss Emma Cummings, typically has a personal identity with the organization and a longer-term perspective than most others. Not only does she know what

the job requires on a day-to-day basis, she very likely understands the traditions and the people of ZYX College, appreciating various employees' contributions and potential. She also may know who likes whom and who does not like whom. Jack would be wise to ask for her input (Prov. 13:10).

3. People may struggle with this question. Since each candidate seems to meet the technical and character requirements of the position, the *prima facie* answer is that Jack would not be wrong no matter which of the three he selected. However, discussants can probe further.

Some may want to rule out Edgar Greene, but they should not do so simply because he is male. His hiring might go against the college's previous tradition of women secretaries, but if he is still fully qualified, it would be illegal to discriminate against his candidacy. Jack Brown will work very closely with his personal executive assistant, however, and he should hire someone who would fit well within the college culture.

Some may consider Amanda Blue's age as a negative factor, but she should not be subjected to age discrimination. Others might consider her age as an advantage, along with her extensive prior experience, because others would perceive that she was hired purely on a merit basis.

Of the three candidates, Cynthia Whyte is the most problematic because of the appearance of possible conflicts of interest. But is this truly a significant factor in this case? According to William Shaw (2005, p. 270) a conflict of interest arises when employees at any level have private interests that are substantial enough to interfere with their job duties; that is, when their private interests lead them, or might reasonably be expected to lead them, to make decisions or act in ways that are detrimental to their employer's interests. The problem may arise from competing financial motivations, but not necessarily; for example, it can involve social and family ties.

Conflicts of interest are morally worrisome not only when an employee acts to the detriment of the organization, but also when the employee's private interests are significant enough to give the appearance of a temptation to act against the company's best interests (Shaw, 2005). A leader should seek to avoid such situations. Full disclosure is always needed, but this often is insufficient.

Because of the spate of well-publicized major corporate scandals (such as those at Enron and Arthur Andersen), business ethics scholars have increasingly focused on this issue (e.g., Carroll and Scherer, 2003; Shaw, 2005; DeGeorge, 2006). The instructor who desires to refer to other cases involving conflicts of interest can direct students to Marianne Jennings's *Business Ethics* (1999) or current cable news programs. Although more dated than her recent casebooks, Jennings' 1999 edition has the greatest variety of such cases.

Avoiding a conflict of interest is especially important for a Christian leader because it can suggest the possibility of impartially or favoritism by the leader, whereas "...God is no respecter of persons" (Acts 10:34b). Even the appearance of a conflict of interest raises clouds as to the motivations in the selection process and can darken the perception of faculty and others as to the motivations of the person hired. Although the executive assistant hired may never intentionally make decisions opposed to the company's interest, adverse perceptions do matter and the leader should thus avoid them. After Jack were to hire Cynthia, if he were to agree with Bernard's recommendation to hire a certain consulting firm, faculty and staff suspicion likely would increase even more. Furthermore, if Cynthia does not work out in the position, Jack would find it particularly awkward to release her because of his close working relationship with Bernard. Most importantly, a God-fearer should treat others impartially and should seek to promote trust. (See Lev. 19:15, Dt. 1:17, Prov. 28:21, 1 Tim. 3:7, and Ti. 1:7)

The culture of an organization often is analogous to that of an extended family. Because of the strategic position and visibility of the assistant, Jack would be ill-advised to hire any spouse or close relative of a subordinate employee or of a board member. This will avoid the appearance of conflicts of interest. Jack should thus not hire Cynthia Whyte if other viable candidates are available.

On the other hand, Jack might contend that, since each of the candidates is technically qualified and has a good character reputation, it would be just and proper for him to choose the one who will provide the best overall support for implementing his honest agenda for the college. Because he does not want to risk offending her husband and because she already has knowledge and contacts within the college community, he might still want to select Cynthia Whyte. As Derry (1991) observes, an act can still be ethical even if it involves mixed motives, if it is good for the organization's interests while also serving the leader's self-interests. Doesn't Christ's commandment to love one's neighbor as oneself mean that it is okay to make prudential decisions? Indeed, most people's motivations are a complex mix of self-interest, altruism, and other influences. Nevertheless, a Christian leader is wise to consider the advice of Joseph Butler in his "Self-deceit" (1726) regarding human nature:

> There is not anything, relating to men and characters, more surprising and unaccountable, than this partiality to themselves, which is observable in many; as there is nothing of more melancholy reflection, respecting morality, virtue, and religion. Hence it is that many men seem perfect strangers to their own characters. They think and reason, and judge quite differently upon any matter relating to themselves, from what they do in cases of others where they are not interested. (pp. 398-399)

Humans tend to avoid serious self-examination. It is more difficult for humans, even Christians, to recognize a potential conflict of interest that involves themselves than it is to recognize conflicts of interest involving others. Jack Brown well might have difficulty seeing the potential problems in hiring Cynthia. This is why he needs to be wise in carefully analyzing himself and in seeking wise counsel. He needs to avoid making a decision that could be perceived by others as self-serving and involving favoritism, one generating undue pressure or temptation for the person he hires. Jack should not bow to his personal desire to hire Cynthia in order to strengthen his good relationship with Bernard.

4. Whom should President Brown select as his first choice? Based on the information stated in the case, Jack should feel comfortable selecting either Edgar Greene or Amanda Blue. Perhaps the wise counsel of others, including Emma Cummings, would help. Like all decisions of a Christian, the most important source of guidance is prayer in line with rational meditation on Scripture.

CASE 2: The President Meets the Faculty

The Bucolic College community was excited when the board of trustees announced its new president, Dr. Stanley Nash. Over the past decade, this small Christian liberal arts college had seen three presidents come and go, and also experienced intervening periods when one of the senior professors had doubled as interim president. The faculty, most long-serving, were ready for more stable leadership.

Although he had no previous experience as a college president, Dr. Nash made a very favorable impression on the faculty when he spoke in chapel during the search process. The search committee recommended him very strongly over several other candidates. He seemed to have new ideas that could ignite growth in enrollment, vigorously expand the program outreach, and revitalize advancement efforts, all needed if the college were to reestablish its financial health. The faculty thus endorsed hiring Dr. Nash.

Prior to assuming his new presidential responsibilities, Dr. Nash met as frequently as he could with available college trustees as well as mentors that he most trusted from past experience. He kept in close contact with faculty members of the search committee, having already established good relations with them. He also decided to meet with each faculty member and key administrator individually during the month prior to his official start at Bucolic College. He hoped to develop his initial strategy and agenda based on these meetings and his own research.

The faculty were eager to meet their new president, especially since the last three presidents had remained aloof from academic concerns. Most, if not all, were glad to share their sense of calling and hopes for their careers and departments. As their comfort levels increased, some also decided to alert the new president of problems as they saw them. Some of these problems they associated with specific faculty members and administrators.

A few of the senior faculty particularly focused their complaints on leadership weaknesses they saw in the academic dean. When she was hired, her principal charge was to assure that Bucolic College would retain its full academic accreditation. To accomplish this, she had instituted new policies regarding tenured faculty review, assessment planning and monitoring, and faculty qualifications. Moreover, she encouraged some popular faculty to leave because of their marginal credentials. She even insisted that some long-time faculty, including a department chair, enroll in terminal degree programs. Some faculty members disagreed with the dean's reforms, thinking them too bureaucratic and onerous for such a small institution.

The regional agency did renew accreditation of the college. The dean believed that this would not have been the case without the unpopular policies she had instituted. Furthermore, she advised the new president that the accrediting agency was now applying even more rigorous standards. The college needed to give even more attention to mission planning and assessment to prepare properly for its next review.

A few months after taking over as president, Dr. Nash terminated the academic dean, replacing her with one of the faculty members who had been most vocal in objecting to her. Some on the faculty were shocked because they admired the professionalism and Christian witness of their now former dean.

The next academic dean replaced the assessment forms designed by his predecessor. However, a year later, because much confusion had been generated by his revision, he reintroduced basically the same forms that the previous dean had used. His tenure as dean was short-lived; he resigned several years prior to the next accreditation review, in which the college fared very poorly.

QUESTIONS:

1. What was inappropriate or inadequate about the new president's process of meeting the faculty and identifying their concerns? What else might he have done?

2. Did the new president underestimate the political realities of a college's culture, even when the members of the culture are professing Christians? What else could he have done to manage these realities?

3. Did the president decide to terminate the academic dean too quickly? His action was legal but was it ethical?

CASE 3: Hitting the Wall

Any person holding a full-time faculty position at an accredited college or university has achieved significant success, often with distinction and certainly with the gratifying recognition of her peers. However, no matter how easy or difficult her career path has been, it is likely that at some time she will face a deflating challenge, one that makes her feel that she has hit a wall. Such a negative experience arises from: being blocked from tenure for political reasons, learning that the administration has decided to cancel the major in her field, or, after being promoted to dean, realizing that the pressing new responsibilities and expectations of the dark side seem to be challenging her capabilities, her comfort zone, or even her moral character. Whatever the cause or situation, hitting the wall can be traumatic and demands serious personal and professional reassessment. To avoid sinking into mental and spiritual depression, a person often needs to make a major decision as to her calling when she hits the wall.

A Christian who had left a successful business career to follow his sense of calling to teach Business Ethics relates his hitting the wall crisis—and its resolution.

> Realizing that I needed an earned doctorate to continue in my new career as a college faculty member, I applied and was accepted to a graduate program as a mature student. I resigned from my junior faculty position at a Christian liberal arts college, declined a full-time call from a small church where I had been supply preaching, sold our house, stored our furniture, and went to Europe to study. Finances were tight although my wife was able to work sporadically as a temp and I worked as a consultant and secured a tuition-reducing grant.
>
> My first term of doctoral studies was very demanding. I worked diligently but was struggling to keep up

with my courses and thesis-related research. My wife, who had left her home and our former financial security, challenged me for falling asleep in church one Sunday, missing a great sermon (she said) by one of the world's most renowned preachers. I prayed fervently for a solution. I started to question whether I should be so far from home and in so different an environment—did I misinterpret God's calling? My hitting a wall challenged my faith and forced a decision.

Scriptural passages on Sabbath observation popped out at me. This seemed to be all I could think about. How could this be God's answer? I was having to study and write papers seven days a week but was barely keeping above water. Not working on Sunday could be disastrous. But I finally submitted, deciding to trust God instead of continuing to question Him.

To my surprise, I started to catch up and earned excellent marks. My weeks became easier and I came to anticipate the Sabbath with relish. I missed some Saturday social events and had to budget my time carefully, but this was not really to my disadvantage. While other students worked hard on Sundays, my wife and I attended worship, took long walks, and enjoyed church music programs. This proved to be a witness that seemed rather strange to other students. After my wife had to return to the U. S. to care for her terminally ill mother, the Sabbath became even more restful and spiritually refreshing for me as I continued fruitfully toward graduation.

God honored my obedience and I have maintained the Sabbath free of work ever since. I remain grateful to God's patience and mercy toward a stubborn sinner like me. (1 John 5:3). (Whetstone, 2006)

Hitting the wall is not an experience exclusive to academics, of course. A successful businessman relates his personal struggle that provides an apt description of this seeming universal challenge.

> When I was in my late 40's, I was given the opportunity to be president of a small instrument company that was struggling in a tough economy. I had to do more firing than hiring. It was obvious, given the unfavorable economic climate, that I would need to be the last one shutting off the power after handing all the employees, great and small, their walking papers. This was the first time I had "hit the wall." Everything I did before this was rather easy and successful. This caused me to seek after Christ all the more. I recall literally wrestling with God in a hotel room in Japan all night. At the end of that exhausting night, I realized that I had to resign for the sake of my family and my sanity.

Author's Note: "Hitting the Wall" is based on a case provided by Dr. Stanley Baczek, Dean of the School of Natural and Applied Sciences, Cedarville University.

QUESTIONS:

1. Describe a time when you hit the wall in your professional career. How has your faith helped you resolve this situation?

2. How did you grow because of the experience?

3. How has this affected what you do and what you avoid doing as a leader?

Chapter Five

Cases Involving the Provost and Deans and Chairs

The provost or academic dean is a key protagonist in the cases of chapter five, especially in her professional relationships with department chairs and other faculty. Case 4 "Full-time Adjuncts," Case 5 "Termination of a Christian Employee," Case 6 "The In-group of True Believers," and Case 7 "An Open Door Policy" feature only a small sampling of the wide variety of issues, great and small, that faculty raise to their provosts and academic deans.

CASE 4: Full-time Adjuncts

Every leader is also a follower, subordinate to God as the spiritual sovereign and most likely also a subordinate to a board, owners, laws and government regulations, and often to a direct report in his organization. Scripture commands every person to render to all what is due them (Rom. 13:7), to obey in all things those who are one's masters on earth, and to work heartily as if working for the Lord (Col. 3:22-23). But what if one's leader orders him to perform a task that appears unethical? Or what if he directs that a task be achieved in an unethical manner? Peter and the apostles answered the high priest who ordered them to halt teaching the gospel of Christ with "we must obey God rather than men" (Acts 5:29). The ethic of "whatever the boss says is right, so I will do it" is inadequate. At times, the Christian may have to decide whether he should simply comply or object to his workplace superior's order because this would not be consistent with working heartily for the Lord. In the public sphere, a loyal citizen might choose civil disobedience. However, one must always be willing to accept the consequences, including any lawful penalties for such willful disobedience of rightful authority.

Even in Christian institutions, ethical dilemmas can be frequent occurrences; they are not merely philosophic abstractions. Busy administrators, committed to achieving their mission responsibilities, can sometimes create ethical challenges for others when acting pragmatically to address a pressing problem. But what should a subordinate, such as a department chairperson, do if he perceives an ethical issue that apparently is not noticed by his dean?

For example, when the accrediting agency examining a Christian university determined that the undergraduate classes were disproportionately taught by part-time adjunct instructors rather than by full-time faculty, the dean implemented a new program that offered contracts to selected adjunct faculty to teach a full load of courses for complete academic years. The full-time adjuncts were not required to fulfill the non-classroom responsibilities that were normally expected of full-time faculty, such as committee assignments, administrative duties, student advising, faculty and student recruiting, and attendance at all university ceremonies. They were paid the adjunct rate for the courses they taught and were not eligible for the healthcare and other benefits paid to full-time faculty. The university chose to include the hours taught by these full-time adjuncts among those reported for full-time instructors in reports to the accrediting agency.

The dean asked the undergraduate department chairs to identify candidates for full-time adjunct contracts from among their team of proven adjunct instructors. Dr. Beige, a department chairperson, found that one of his adjunct instructors was willing to sign such a contract. But Dr. Beige had misgivings; he did not know whether the accrediting agency had agreed to the use of the new contracts or was even aware of them, but he felt that the students might be disadvantaged. His concern was not about a reduction in the quality of the class instruction but by the more intangible possible deficiency of extra-classroom faculty support, versus that possible from on-site full-time faculty. Moreover, the ones designated *full-time adjuncts* would not receive the benefits of regular full-time faculty. He wondered whether using the full-time adjuncts would really be fair to the students or to the adjuncts.

On the other hand, the dean's new arrangement eliminated a stumbling block to accreditation without increasing faculty expense or significantly reducing the quality of class instruction. Since the other department chairs were either not concerned or unwilling to express any objection, Dr. Beige feared that he would appear negative if he questioned this new policy, either in a faculty meeting or privately with the dean. He wondered whether or not his vocal opposition would diminish the dean's trust in him, a dire consequence since the dean held a veto over his upcoming tenure review and future compensation.

QUESTIONS:

1. Assess ethically the new program concerning full-time adjunct faculty. What issues are raised from the perspectives of consequential utilitarianism, rights, justice, and character or virtue ethics?

2. To whom (which stakeholder groups) should the administration communicate its decision to adopt the new full-time adjuncts policy?

3. Should Dr. Beige, the concerned chair, voice his objections? If so, to whom and in what manner?

4. If the chair remained unconvinced as to the ethical soundness of the full-time adjunct program, could he really trust the honesty of the dean in the future?

5. If the full-time adjunct faculty program is implemented without addressing his concerns, what should Dr. Beige do?

CASE 5: Termination of a Christian Employee

PART I

Mr. Abe Farmer was the Director of Institutional Research for a small Christian liberal arts college in an employment-at-will state. After the new college president appointed a new academic dean, Mr. Farmer attempted to meet with the dean, his immediate supervisor. He was naturally concerned to confirm his relationship and the dean's expectations for him. The new dean was extremely busy learning her new job but scheduled a meeting with him on a Monday at the end of her first month's service.

At this meeting, the dean assigned four major data research and assessment projects to Mr. Farmer, giving him a deadline for the following Thursday, three days after their initial meeting. Mr. Farmer asked Information Technology for access to some of the data needed to complete his assignment but was told by the Director of Information Technology that his staff were busy with other agenda and were thus unable to work with him that week. Mr. Farmer reported this hurdle to the dean on Tuesday. The dean immediately telephoned the Director of Information Technology, who responded with the data needed for the analysis in less than an hour. The dean brusquely informed Mr. Farmer of this, seemingly questioning his competence.

Mr. Farmer, less than two years from retirement, was a Christian committed to serving the college's mission of educating students intellectually, spiritually, physically, and emotionally to be servant leaders. Mr. Farmer had been hired by the previous dean and had labored at the college for several years. Although he had a previous record of success in strategic planning and assessment, his efforts had not yet borne significant fruit at this college. His recommendations had received little genuine support from the previous president or the majority of the faculty, who considered planning and assessment as distractions from their more critical roles as teachers and mentors of students. Nevertheless,

Mr. Farmer had always received favorable job performance reviews and developed warm friendships with the previous dean, other administrators, and some faculty members.

Mr. Farmer worked diligently to complete his four assignments by the Thursday deadline, feeling he was making some substantial progress. However, when he reported for work as usual on Thursday morning he found a letter from the dean on his desk. In a terse statement the letter informed Mr. Farmer of his termination as of that day, the last day of the month. He was instructed to clean out his office by the end of the next day.

QUESTIONS:

1. Was the dean's assignment and the manner in which it was supported a fair test? What additional communication and support by the dean and other involved parties might have led to a more God-honoring outcome?

2. Was Mr. Farmer treated ethically? Explain your answer based on consequentialist, rights, justice, and virtue approaches to ethical analysis.

3. Should avowedly Christian institutions relate to its Christian employees in any way beyond legal requirements? If so, in what ways? Explain.

CASE 5: Termination of a Christian Employee (continued)

PART II

Rosa Prospect was a non-tenured faculty member who taught management, organizational behavior, and ethics at the college where Mr. Farmer worked. Prior to returning to graduate school to earn her doctorate, she had worked on the corporate planning staff of a multinational corporation where she experienced first-hand some of the challenges and frustrations of working with busy, strong-willed managers and executives. She had found that they sometimes resist the challenging and time-consuming work of strategic planning because they are consumed with meeting the goals set for them in their own areas of responsibility.

While at the college, Rosa had become acquainted with Mr. Farmer and come to respect his Christian testimony and his commitment to the mission of the college, especially regarding planning and assessment. She was surprised when the dean announced that Mr. Farmer was leaving, so she spoke to him and with several colleagues about concern for him. Although she did not conduct any deliberate investigation, she gradually learned enough to piece together his case, to the extent summarized in Part I.

Dr. Prospect concluded that Mr. Farmer may not have been treated justly regarding the manner and circumstances of his termination. Moreover, as she had been teaching her course in ethics she had observed that her students tended to grow more cynical when they perceived that administrative decisions were made pragmatically rather than according to the principles of rights, justice, and Christian virtues she was promoting. As she wrote a letter of recommendation for Mr. Farmer and prayed for him and the college, she wondered what else she might have done, based on her information of his situation.

QUESTIONS:

1. Which of the following action(s) should Dr. Prospect have taken?

   a. Accepted the outcome as being best for all concerned, and thus moved on
   b. Scheduled a meeting with the dean to communicate her concerns
   c. Raised her concerns by asking the dean for an explanation at the next faculty meeting
   d. Written a letter to the college president with her questions and concerns
   e. Written a case on the termination of Mr. Farmer and used it for faculty and class discussion
   f. Decided that her most prudent action was to leave the college and seek other employment

2. Explain the positive and negative consequences of her decision—for Dr. Prospect and for the college.

3. How could Dr. Prospect defend her decision in terms of rights, justice, and virtue?

CASE 6: The In-group of True Believers

Greenlake College is a small Christian liberal arts college founded at the beginning of the twentieth century. It is fully accredited and has developed a significant role in its region, evidenced by the contributions of its graduates to business, the arts, the professions, and Christian ministry and missions. Nevertheless, having no significant denominational support or public funding, it has periodically struggled financially. Over the past decade its enrollment has stagnated and its finances have deteriorated, necessitating that its annual budget shortfall be met by a dwindling number of key donors.

Alumni consider the faculty to be a strength of the college's academic program. A number of the departments, all small, are chaired by career faculty who have taught at Greenlake for over twenty years. Many were originally hired during a building phase led by a president who had a public school background. Their long dedication to their calling to teach for relatively low financial reward is generally recognized by alumni, students, administration, and the trustees. Former students often maintain contact with their favorite professors, who seem to relish recounting their students' life accomplishments at faculty meetings. However, some alumni who are now members of nearby churches feel strongly that over the last two decades the college has drifted away from its Christian mission because the admittedly capable old-time faculty are not committed enough to faith integration.

Greenlake College indeed has struggled in recent years over its mission and identity. Is its primary role to prepare Christians for service in Christ's Church and Kingdom or is it to focus on excellent liberal arts education for the broader community? More graphically, one group wants Greenlake to become more of a regional beacon for Christ-centered integration of faith and learning, and the other wants to stress academic excellence while avoiding the taint of being too much of a Bible college. Supporters of both views feel that the college cannot do both simultaneously due to its size and financial condition, and the board of trustees has offered no consensus opinion as to the right future direction for Greenlake.

The new college president, a former Greenlake professor and a pastor, is well aware of the identity problem. His efforts to elicit greater support from nearby churches are proving only moderately successful because some church members are critical of the decline of the college's Christian witness. The board of trustees, led by increasingly weary major donors, expects the president to develop a strategy that will eliminate the chronic financial deficits.

The president commissions a faculty member to develop a strategic plan for the college, but this exercise primarily concludes that the president must first decide on what direction to take. He decides to reinforce Greenlake's Christian mission as the college's primary priority. He appoints a new provost who has been a teacher in the Bible Department, a man who has lobbied for requiring greater biblical integration throughout the curriculum. The new provost also seems to have innovative, cost effective ideas for enhancing the college's recruiting and management processes.

One of the initial steps the new provost takes is to call a meeting of a select group of the faculty, those he has identified as committed to greater faith integration. At this meeting he commends them for their Christian testimony and dedication. He explains that they are the nucleus for the revitalization of Greenlake as a Christ-centered college. This will require them to revise the curriculum to achieve greater integration of faith and learning. He intends to continue to meet with this core group to plan how this best can be accomplished. He requests that they not discuss these meetings with other faculty and staff, at least not during the initial planning phase.

The faculty members at this meeting ask only a few questions. Assistant Professor Duane Johnson does ask if there are other faculty members who will be in this planning group but who were unable to come to this initial meeting. The provost responds that everyone invited is present. Although Duane Johnson agrees with the aim of enhancing Christian integration and learning across the curriculum, he still feels uneasy. Having become well acquainted with several of the older faculty as personal colleagues, he considers them to be Christians who love the college and the students. He recognizes that they had never been trained in teaching from a Christian worldview and that they might tend to segregate their subject matter from their own faith positions. But he wonders whether it is right and just to exclude them from planning, essentially establishing an out-group of faculty and a separate in-group exclusively tasked for such a critically important effort, one that will affect everyone's career.

As the meeting ends and the other in-group faculty are leaving, Duane approaches the provost to request politely that he be allowed to resign from this select planning group. But before he gets the provost's attention, he has some second thoughts. He is still a junior faculty member who is coming up for tenure this year. Moreover, if he leaves the planning group, he will probably lose any opportunity he has to influence the strategic changes and the planning that will affect his own department.

QUESTIONS:

1. Should Duane Johnson resign from the in-group at this time, at the end of the initial meeting of the select group? Or should he postpone his decision in order to weigh the consequences more fully against his initial moral judgment? Should he also consult respected counselors?

2. If he does request to be removed from the select committee, would Duane be properly respecting the legitimate authority of the

provost? How might the provost respond, to the request and toward Duane in the future?

CASE 7: An Open Door Policy

Appointment of a new president, provost, or academic dean is a major event for any college or university. It brings hopeful expectations, but it can also be unsettling as faculty and staff speculate as to the changes the new leader will make. Some rumblings due to uncertainty were heard at Alphaomega Christian University following the appointment of a new provost, Dr. Hiram Baker, who had come from a public institution. But after Dr. Baker's first meeting with the assembled faculty, Dr. Timothy Mason agreed with his colleagues that the provost had laid a good foundation for future relationships when he gave his personal Christian testimony and announced that he would have an open door policy as he got to know and learn from his fellow faculty members. Applying his outgoing personality, Provost Baker met with individuals, visited all of the university's schools and departments, and invited faculty to make appointments with him to discuss their own areas and career interests.

Several months later, Dr. Baker announced that the board of trustees had asked him to propose ideas for restructuring the university to streamline its operations. He emphasized that a major objective of the restructuring was cost reduction and offered an open invitation to the faculty to contribute their ideas and suggestions.

When Dr. Baker met with the faculty of arts and sciences, he reiterated his appeal for suggestions although he had to leave for another appointment before these could be discussed. Dr. Mason, a department chair, asked him if he would be interested in reading his paper on the purposes of Christian higher education. The provost agreed enthusiastically, responding that it might provide insights for the restructuring process.

In a few weeks Dr. Baker appointed a special faculty committee to audit the university's programs and departments. It would also research structures employed at other universities and recommend a new academic structure for Alphaomega Christian. Although Dr. Mason asked to serve on this university committee and had served on similar committees in business and other colleges, he was not among those selected. After a few months he and other faculty eventually were asked to review an initial draft of the special committee's report. He did so but was provided no additional information and told that the provost was insisting that the special committee's future work be kept confidential. Rumors of major changes increased along the grapevine for a time but subsided as the faculty addressed their normal responsibilities.

After Dr. Baker had been at Alphaomega Christian for a year, the registrar announced a new policy relating to minimum class size. The minimum for any class was increased to ten students from the previous cut-off of seven. Dr. Mason was concerned because students frequently complained when courses, especially those meeting degree requirements, were canceled immediately prior to a term. When cancellations necessitated postponement of their graduation dates, students sometimes asked for directed studies. University policy, however, strongly discouraged use of directed studies and did not offer faculty compensation for teaching them.

Dr. Mason realized that the tuition-driven university needed to maintain average class sizes that would cover all marginal costs and a reasonable allocation of fixed university overheads. Nevertheless, he felt that at least a few classes could be offered each term if demanded by enough students to cover the additional or marginal costs—primarily adjunct instructor compensation—even if they did not generate enough student revenue to also cover all of the normal allocation of university fixed costs. Such classes, in fact, would actually offer at least some contribution to overheads while further meeting students' course needs.

He developed a simple mathematical model that clearly demonstrated that a class size as small as three students would more than cover the compensation of its instructor. However, since three students is generally too few for group assignments, he developed a recommendation that five students be established as the minimum class size for one or a few additional classes each term. These would provide a valuable service to students who needed these extra courses. Moreover, even if these additional class sections enrolled only five to nine students, the resulting tuition would contribute positively to net revenues and increase the total profit of the university.

Taking up the provost's offer to meet individually with faculty, Dr. Mason called for an appointment. Dr. Baker agreed to a time and cordially welcomed Dr. Mason at the meeting. He asked Dr. Mason to describe his background and commitment to his calling to teach at Alphaomega Christian and complimented him on his paper on Christian higher education. However, he did not comment on the ongoing planning for academic reorganization of the university. The professor also gave the provost a copy of his brief analysis of minimum class size and suggested that he would appreciate comments on it. Dr. Baker thanked him and promised to read it after their meeting.

Dr. Mason did not have the opportunity to talk with Dr. Baker for some time thereafter since the provost was extremely busy. When their paths crossed on campus, the provost always expressed greetings or waved but never seemed to have time to stop to chat. At the periodic faculty assemblies, the provost reiterated his desire for participation but offered no substantive information on the restructuring process or any other faculty suggestions.

Dr. Mason was neither surprised nor overly concerned that he heard no further about his minimum class size suggestion, but was somewhat disappointed when the registrar rigidly enforced the minimum size of ten students in the next class scheduling cycle, emphasizing that the provost had directed her to do so.

The professor did become concerned, however, when he was soon thereafter removed from several committee assignments and given no new ones. Instead, additional assignments seemed to favor the members of the provost's special university committee, even though their final report remained unpublished.

Dr. Mason's dean, who met with the provost weekly, also seemed to have adapted a cooler attitude toward the professor. Though she had previously made an effort to publicly praise his qualifications and contributions to the university, she was no longer soliciting his opinions in faculty meetings; she criticized his department publicly; and she neglected to include his faculty accomplishments, such as presentation of papers at conferences and publications, when she listed those of others.

QUESTIONS:

1. Based on the case account, why might Dr. Mason's dean have changed her attitude toward him?

2. Was Dr. Mason out of line in offering his ideas about Christian higher education and minimum class size to the new provost? Assess the manner in which he offered his suggestions.

3. What does Dr. Mason's experience indicate about the true nature of the provost's open door policy? How successful do you think it will prove to be in encouraging innovation and entrepreneurship among the faculty as a whole?

4. How could the provost have better handled his relationship with talented and engaged faculty members like Dr. Mason, while retaining the professor's morale and confidence?

Chapter Six

Cases Involving Chairs and Faculty

Case 8 "Investigation of MBA Programs" and Case 9 "The Special Lady," present faculty department chairs in the primary decision-making role. Higher administrators and other faculty are also involved and can expect to face similar issues at their levels.

CASE 8: Investigation of MBA Programs

Thomas Young is a senior majoring in Business Administration who also plays third base on the college's baseball team. He comes from a Christian family and has taken his studies as well as his baseball seriously throughout his undergraduate career, maintaining a solid B+ average. Dr. Gray, chair of the business administration department, is rather surprised when Thomas comes to his office during the final week of the term with a concern about his marketing research class. Thomas explains that he has done well in this course to date, but he is unsure that he can complete the major project assignment for this class.

The instructor of the marketing research class is Bob Smith, a manager in the Christian college's advancement office and a doctoral student in marketing, who is teaching in Dr. Gray's department for the first time, having been highly recommended by the college president. Dr. Gray remembers that the academic dean recently informed his chairs that the president had asked Bob to prepare a recommendation to the college council as to the marketing feasibility of a new MBA program.

Thomas explains to Dr. Gray that the major project assignment requires each class member to visit another of the nearby colleges that offer MBA degree programs. Students are expected to represent themselves as prospective applicants for the upcoming fall. They are to find out all they can about the curriculum, facilities, faculty, tuition and fees, and other aspects of the program from the school's representatives and current students. Each of the class members is then to submit a report of findings to Mr. Smith.

Thomas tells Dr. Gray that he has no intention of actually applying to any of the area's MBA programs. He comments that at first he had eagerly embarked on the assignment because it involves practical hands-on experience rather than being just another routine textbook case. But now he is not so sure. He wonders if pretending to have a genuine interest in enrolling in the MBA program is actually equivalent to lying. But he does not want to hurt his class grade by choosing not to complete the assignment.

Dr. Gray decides to ask Bob Smith about this assignment. Bob says the papers he has received so far are excellent, and he intends to collate the students' findings as an important empirical basis for his report to the college council in support of his recommendation to proceed with an MBA program. He feels that the surreptitious approach taken by the students for data gathering will provide a more accurate assessment than he could gather from the other schools' websites. He anticipates that the student insights can help him identify a strong marketing niche for the college's new program.

QUESTIONS:

1. Is the surreptitious research approach required for the major project assignment ethical? Consider your answer from the consequentialist, rights, justice, and virtue ethics perspectives. If the answer differs depending on which ethics criterion is applied, which one deserves most weight in this case? (For example, if the deception required of the students would be unethical in terms of rights, justice, or virtue, do the anticipated benefits to the college's new MBA program and to its future students outweigh other ethical questions?)

2. How should Dr. Gray counsel student Thomas Young?

3. How should Dr. Gray counsel instructor Bob Smith?

4. What, if any, actions should Dr. Gray take to prevent similar cases in the future?

CASE 9: The Special Lady

Irma Orr was hired five years ago as a tenure track member of the faculty of a Christian college. She has since regularly taught a full load of courses, ones that none of the other faculty members are qualified to offer. Her student evaluations have been very positive. But from her first term she has insisted that she could only manage a full teaching load, while also raising a large family and serving in her church, if she were exempted from non-instructional duties such as committee membership and student advising. Since her courses are critical ones for the students, Dr. Adams, the chair of her department, has accorded her the special treatment she requested.

Now she has applied for tenure with Dr. Adams' full support, even though she has not served on any department or university committees and has been exempted from other normal full-time faculty responsibilities. The departmental tenure committee recognizes that she is receiving special treatment, but its members have not opposed their chair's position on her tenure because of their reluctance to go against him.

Nevertheless, department faculty colleagues sometimes refer to Ms. Orr as "the special lady" and several have recently gone privately to Dr. Adams with complaints about her special privileges. Although he explained to them the importance of offering students the courses she teaches and the lack of success he has had in finding anyone else who is qualified to teach them, he knows they were not totally convinced. He wonders if he is guilty of playing favorites.

Author's Note: "The special lady" is based on a case provided by Dr. Stanley Baczek, Dean, School of Natural and Applied Sciences, Cedarville University.

QUESTIONS:

1. What are the political and ethical subtleties of this situation?

2. How should Dr. Adams, as department chair, handle the tenure situation of Ms. Orr, "The special lady"?

3. What preventative steps should Dr. Adams have taken earlier in the process?

4. What steps should Dr. Adams, or the academic dean, now take to avoid similar situations in the future?

Chapter Seven

Cases Involving Contested Grades

Challenges to student grades is an unpleasant but seemingly ubiquitous issue. Case 10 is "The Threatening Father," and Case 11 is "The Aspiring Academic All-American." The course instructor and department chair are most immediately involved, but special cases such as these can and do sometimes bring in the president, provost, and deans.

CASE 10: The Threatening Father

Chair Dr. James Gold is rather surprised when he receives a message to call the college president. As he is picking up his phone, one of the untenured faculty in the department, Sarah Green, comes into his office. She warns him that one of her students is appealing her grade on a final examination. Sarah had previously informed him that the student had cheated on the exam by texting an exam question to another student. He agreed that she had correctly awarded the student a grade of zero on the exam. Because of the large weighting of the exam, the student also failed the course.

Dr. Gold checks with the registrar and learns that the student has already submitted a form to appeal her grade, claiming that she had not cheated. As department chair, Dr. Gold decides to continue to support the accusation made by Sarah Green and the failing grade she assigned to the student.

However, when he talks with the president, Dr. Gold learns that the accused student's parents have contacted the president in support of their daughter's appeal. The president informs him that the student's father is a substantial donor and is very influential in his mega-church in the primary market area served by the college. He is threatening to blacklist the college if his daughter's grade is not changed to a passing mark so she will receive full credit for the course. Moreover, he is demanding that Sarah Green withdraw her accusation of cheating and make a personal apology to his daughter. The father demands that Sarah's employment be terminated if she does not change the grade and apologize.

Author's Note: "The Threatening Father" is based on a case provided by Dr. Stanley Baczek, Dean, School of Natural and Applied Sciences, Cedarville University.

QUESTIONS:

1. What are the political, legal, and ethical issues raised in this case? What biblical principles apply?

2. What should Dr. Gold do? What decision should he make and what specific steps should he take to implement it?

3. If the president wants to appease the donor, instructing Dr. Gold to ask Sarah Green to apologize to the student, can he, as chairperson, comply in a creative way that will preserve his professional integrity? Explain.

CASE 11: The Aspiring Academic All-American

Dr. Henry Branch loves both philosophy and baseball. Since God gifted him much more in the capabilities required for the former than for the latter, he had accepted a faculty position teaching philosophy at a small Christian liberal arts college. He nevertheless attended as many games as possible involving the college's teams, especially those of the baseball team.

He strived to instill in the players a commitment to be scholar athletes. Very few of the small college's student athletes would ever become professional players, although a surprising number expressed a desire to do so. Dr. Branch encouraged the players to apply to their academic studies and careers the lessons they were learning about teamwork and the need for dedicated preparation for athletic competitions. He felt this was an especially important role for him since some of the faculty appeared to bring a negative perception of athletes to the classroom. As chair of the faculty athletic committee, he learned that many of the student athletes believed that this bias was factual, with some faculty merely tolerating them and their coaches merely because the college needed to offer intercollegiate sports as an enrollment strategy. Dr. Branch wanted to counter such perceptions or misconceptions, which he felt were unhealthy for the culture of the college.

Charlie Jones, star second baseman of the college baseball team, was a fine example of a scholar athlete. By his senior year he became team captain. Throughout his first three years as a student, he proved to be diligent, ranking in the upper portion of his classes in core subjects as well as in his major. He planned to enroll in an MBA program at a state university after completing his bachelor's degree. He also exhibited strong moral character, drawing on his upbringing in his Christian home. He had an outgoing personality, often dropping by to see Dr. Branch and other instructors to discuss subjects brought up in class and their implications for his career plans.

Near the end of the fall semester of his senior year, Charlie came by to discuss the final examination in an advanced course taught by Dr. Branch. Charlie explained that he wanted to earn an A in the course and asked what he needed to do to raise his current B+ class average. He hoped to be recognized as an Academic All-American. But he was worried that he would not be if he did not receive an A for this course.

Dr. Branch was delighted to hear about Charlie's good prospects for becoming an Academic All-American. This would be a great honor for Charlie and would publicly vindicate the professor's efforts on behalf of athletes as worthy scholars. Dr. Branch assured Charlie that if he scored in the A range on his final examination, he would receive an A for the course. This was not an exception made for Charlie, however. Dr. Branch gave comprehensive final examinations and made a point of informing the entire class that his policy was to award as the final course grade either the final examination grade or the grade based on all course work including the final, whichever was highest. He anticipated that Charlie would make an A on the final and thus for the course, based on both his proven ability to do so and his special incentive to become an Academic All-American.

However, Charlie made a B- on his final examination, and Dr. Branch awarded him the grade of B for the course. Based on past experience, he knew that his chair would support his grading decisions. Nevertheless, he grieved that this grade might well prevent Charlie from becoming an Academic All-American.

Charlie no longer dropped by Dr. Branch's office to chat and avoided him for the rest of his senior year.

QUESTIONS:

1. Did Dr. Branch act appropriately regarding Charlie's grade? What else, if anything, should he have done to improve Charlie's chances of making Academic All-American?

2. Should Dr. Branch have proactively tried to reestablish good communication with Charlie? If so, explain how.

3. If Charlie did become an Academic All-American the following spring, in spite of his grade in Dr. Branch's course, would you change your answers to the previous questions?

Chapter Eight

Case Involving Outside Consultants

Case 12 "The Consultant Who Felt Bilked" is the sole case in this chapter. A dean and a faculty chair are the key actors although it also involves contractual relationships with an outside party. It thus is only one situation representing a variety of issues that require institutional policies with potential legal and public relations impacts.

CASE 12: The Consultant Who Felt Bilked

Ms. Jane Purple, the interim academic dean of FWU, an accredited mid-sized Christian university, was confronted with simultaneous pressures from her superiors. She was advised to: (1) tightly control her modest expense budget, and (2) increase undergraduate enrollment rapidly. She initially had accepted the interim dean position only reluctantly because she was not credentialed as an academic. Nevertheless, she was assured by the provost that she had gained the trust and support of top university administrators because of her marketing expertise and her prior successful management of an administrative department.

Ms. Purple quickly moved to implement cost conserving measures and revamped expense reporting policies to address the first pressure. To address the second, she hired more recruiters and increased advertising expenditures to boost enrollment. Realizing that even this intensified effort might not realize her aggressive growth goals, she also pressed academic department heads to increase course offerings, majors, and minors. A particularly promising new area was healthcare administration, a rapidly expanding occupational field that several members of the board of trustees, as well as the larger hospital groups in the region, had suggested to FWU's chancellor. He personally contacted Ms. Purple to investigate this area, one that would help FWU expand its enrollment while enhancing its service to the community. Not surprisingly, Ms. Purple decided to push for healthcare administration, requesting Dr. Milton White, Department Chair of Management, to develop an undergraduate program on a high priority basis.

Dr. White agreed that healthcare administration offered promise, but he was concerned because none of the current faculty had experience or credentials in this field. Nevertheless, he reluctantly agreed to assume the lead in developing the required curriculum. And from the outset he urged his superior to hire a fully-qualified academic in healthcare administration who could take over direct responsibility for finalizing and implementing the new curriculum program.

Dr. White began by researching the field to prepare a proposal that could meet the standards for formal approval by FWU's curriculum review committee. Once approved and included in the catalog, the program curriculum could serve as the basis for student recruitment and for hiring a full-time academic to complete development of the courses, recruit instructors, and otherwise develop and direct the program in compliance with accreditation requirements.

As an experienced course and program developer, Dr. White understood that his lack of expertise in healthcare administration would require him to draw on experienced and knowledgeable people from outside the university. He conducted exploratory library research, consulted informally with friends having experience designing healthcare curricula, and arranged to meet with administrators of hospitals within the region. One contact suggested hiring Ms. Green, a local healthcare manager who held degrees in both business and healthcare administration, as a consultant. Ms. Green agreed to critique the work already begun and to recommend a good market niche for FWU. Dr. White also hoped that Ms. Green would, after the initial study, be able to help identify adjunct teacher candidates and possibly personally develop courses and teach for the new program. Not having the necessary funds in his department budget, Dr. White recommended that the Dean Purple interview Ms. Green as a consultant. The dean readily agreed to set up a meeting for this purpose.

Prior to the meeting, Dr. White learned that Ms. Green was an alumna of FWU, where she had earned her MBA. He felt that it was good that the consultant already was familiar with the school, its curriculum, and business faculty. However, he considered that her healthcare and management education, professional experience, and research background justified her hire, in any case.

Dean Purple began the meeting by allowing and encouraging each person present to share backgrounds and interests, promoting a congenial, positive environment for conducting the business at hand. She then asked Dr. White to explain the university's hopes for an undergraduate healthcare administration degree program and his progress to date in planning for it. After he did so, the dean requested that Ms. Green describe her qualifications and experience and propose how she might be able to help. Ms. Green responded that she was prepared to write a report with recommendations for (1) the best program for FWU in the regional student market; and (2) specific curriculum proposals and descriptions, based on her analysis of the multifaceted industry populated by healthcare providers and her comparative analysis of the offerings of other universities. Dr. White agreed that these findings would help in deciding how to proceed with program planning, approval, and implementation.

Before agreeing, Dean Purple said she first wanted to understand the specifics that such a report would specifically address. She asked Dr. White what he thought were the most critical questions. Dr. White responded that he still had numerous questions. Would a completely online program suit the regional market? Since no academically qualified healthcare administration professor had yet been hired, was total dependence on qualified part-time adjuncts satisfactory for a successful start-up? Even though some existing management courses would be included in any curriculum, which new healthcare administration courses should, and could, be designed and offered first, in time for program start-up by the following fall term?

Dr. White agreed with the consultant that fewer new courses would be required if, at least for the first few years, the program was offered as a concentration rather than as a separate new major. Graduates would earn the B.S. degree in management with a concentration in healthcare administration. The concentration alternative would reduce initial faculty hiring requirements since Dr. White's doctorate would satisfy accreditation standards. Alternatively, starting the program as a distinct healthcare administration major (B.S.) would require hiring at least one full-time faculty member with a doctorate in this field before courses could be offered. The supply of qualified candidates was much lower than the demand, meaning that the recruiting process could prove long and require paying the successful candidate considerably more than the university's current scale. Given the recent budget cutbacks, paying a high salary to a new faculty member might undermine the morale of existing faculty. Of course, a concentration option must meet the needs of prospective students or the new program would fail.

Ms. Green confirmed her willingness to address all of these questions in her study. Dean Purple then asked Ms. Green to submit something in writing within two weeks, working with the help and information that Dr. White could supply. Dr. White interpreted the dean to be asking Ms. Green, as a consultant, to prepare a detailed study report proposal, including preliminary findings and recommendations for additional work needed to address all the issues thoroughly. He noted that the dean had not brought up any discussion of fees nor was a contract signed. He agreed to work with Ms. Green by providing the additional information she requested.

Two weeks later, Ms. Green sent Dean Purple and Dr. White copies of her 20-page report. The dean asked Dr. White to provide her an assessment and to recommend if FWU should continue to use Ms. Green as a consultant.

Dr. White found the report to be comprehensive for a preliminary report, clearly and rationally addressing the major questions and concerns raised at the previous meeting. The industry review, including descriptions of various types of healthcare providers and employment opportunities for future graduates, augmented the literature search he had initially conducted. The report also listed the Healthcare programs offered by other universities in the region and identified the principal competitors FWU would face. Drawing primarily on the prospective curriculum plans provided her by Dr. White, the report recommended course descriptions for the required courses, both for a possible major and the concentration options. Ms. Green recommended the latter, being suitable to the needs of potential students and easier to implement on a short time schedule.

With her report Ms. Green included a bill for $5,000, reflecting 20 hours at a $250 per hour consulting fee rate. Dr. White was unaware of what, if anything, Dean Purple had agreed to pay Ms. Green. Nevertheless, he was pleased with the comprehensiveness of the report, reflecting considerable productive effort in a relatively short period of time. Ms. Green's recommendations provided important support for decisions that FWU needed to make, although much of the report drew heavily on the information and research findings he had provided her after the initial meeting.

Dr. White reported to the dean that he was pleased with the report but felt that $5,000 was probably too much to pay for it. Dean Purple said she was shocked, actually offended, by the amount billed and would think about what to do about it. Dr. White suggested that Ms. Green deserved compensation for her effort and contributions, at least $1,000-$2,000. However, as a department chair, he did not have the authority or budgeted funds to pay consultants. Payment would have to be left to the dean's determination.

Approximately a week later, the dean asked Dr. White if he still wanted to work with a consultant, continuing with Ms. Green or perhaps hiring someone else. He responded that he did not, that after discussing the report with Ms. Green he now felt confident that he could complete plans for developing the new program, relying on his own industry contacts and further research. Nevertheless, he reminded the dean that the school needed to intensify the search for a fully qualified full-time faculty member to assume direction of course development and actual implementation of the new program.

Over the next few months Dr. White completed the curriculum plan for the option chosen: a management (B.S.) major with a concentration in healthcare administration. For this, he relied heavily on significant information and advice from regional hospital administrators and the Association of University Programs in Health Administration, which certifies undergraduate and graduate programs. FWU's curriculum committee approved Dr. White's curriculum proposal, allowing him to proceed with hiring qualified adjunct instructors for course development. The first course offerings were scheduled for the following term.

Dean Purple chose to postpone any search for full-time faculty for healthcare administration until enough students could be recruited to support the additional expenses involved. And when Dr. White asked her what she had eventually done about compensating Ms. Green for her report, she responded that she had decided not to pay her anything.

QUESTIONS:

1. What amount should the dean have paid Ms. Green?

   a. The $5,000 billed based on consulting hours worked?

   b. A reduced amount of $1,000 to $2,000, as suggested by Dr. White?

   c. Nothing?

2. Was it ethically appropriate for Dr. White to include within his written proposal to the university curriculum committee any statistics and other data introduced by Ms. Green in her report, one for which she received no financial compensation? Would it make a difference if the consultant personally authorized such use?

3. Assess how well the interim dean handled the meeting and business dealings with Ms. Green. Why do you think she did not establish

firm terms of financial compensation with Ms. Green when she requested a report within two weeks?

4. What lessons can be drawn from this case—by consultants and those using them—in terms of hiring and compensating consultants?

5. How might the facts and lessons of this case influence Dr. White in approaching future projects, particularly concerning his interactions with the interim dean?

6. Referring to biblical principles, discuss how a Christian servant leader might act differently from the conduct described for:

   a. Dean Purple
   b. Ms. Green, the consultant
   c. Dr. White

Chapter Nine

Concluding Thoughts on the Use of Cases

Patricia Werhane's (1993) observation that the American business ethics establishment is committed to the case method continues to ring true. Cases can be effective tools for teaching ethical decision-making.

However, total reliance on the case method is insufficient, even detrimental. Ethics teachers often prefer to focus on difficult ethical dilemmas found in cases because they provide interesting and challenging exercises. But focusing on only the most difficult quandaries can mislead students to conclude that there are no right answers to ethical questions. Such a cynical response is unjustified and unfortunate. While cognitively challenging dilemmas can be expected and must be addressed when they occur, they actually represent exceptions to the normal range of problems that daily confront organizational managements.

The cases in this book are based on actual situations, raising ethical issues that are not unsolvable quandaries, but ones that collectively represent the challenges university administrators and faculty can expect and are expected to get right. The twelve cases are meant to provoke discussion without being unsolvable.

Dr. J. Thomas Whetstone

American leaders tend to be pragmatic and relativistic. But a Christian need not be limited to an ethic of relativism. A biblical ethic, while promoting cultural tolerance, teaches that there are limits to such tolerance. Christians believe that God seeks truth and justice while manifesting mercy and grace. This book presumes "the normative view that there are universal moral principles which ought to be regarded as exceptionless in every culture and that the moral rules we adopt should apply those principles to universal areas of concern and activity" (Holmes, 1984, p. 21). Morally superior answers exist and should be sought, with proper appreciation of the diversity of human perspectives and ever with compassion.

Nevertheless, people often rationalize, thereby making ethical analysis more complex than it needs to be. Willfully choosing to do what we know is right is often more difficult than deciding what is the most right thing to do. This requires strength of moral character, especially the reliance on the virtue of practical wisdom (Aristotle's *phronesis* or Aquinas's *prudentia*), which is developed through experience and emulation of moral exemplars. This is the most essential virtue of business leaders (Beabout, 2012) and surely is important for university administrators as well. Ethical decision-making and behavior also requires a person to humbly acknowledge his mortal limitations and to resist temptations and pressures on his sin-impaired will.

Thus, applied ethics involves more than cognitive decision-making. The aims of ethics teaching should include not only (1) raising the students' awareness of the ethical aspects of relationships, situations, and behaviors and (2) equipping them with sound tools for ethical decision-making, but also (3) helping them understand the nature of the ethical person and how he can develop a more virtuous moral character (Whetstone, 2006, p.13). Ethics principles and lessons learned from cases can be very helpful, but growth as a moral leader with "moral common sense" is a development process involving decisions and interactions with others in actually experienced situations and varying contexts (Weaver, 2017).

The majority of this writer's ethics students say that they are more morally uplifted by reading edifying accounts of people demonstrating exemplary character virtues than they are by analyzing and discussing difficult ethical case dilemmas. This consistently has been the testimony of students after they completed a class exercise comparing two stories, "The Heinz Dilemma" (Kohlberg, 1981) and "The Russian Rabbi" (Sommers & Sommers, 2001). In the first, a loving husband has to choose whether or not to steal a dose of an expensive drug that his cancer-infested wife desperately needs. The instructor challenges students to evaluate the husband's decision options based on the most likely consequences of his choice, based on rights and justice to each stakeholder, and as guided by a virtue ethic. Analyzing this difficult dilemma helps students hone their ethical awareness and theoretical understanding as they compare approaches and alternative decision choices. However, according to most students the Heinz Dilemma is not as morally uplifting as the second story, a simple account of a Russian rabbi who each Friday morning disappears to cut and gather firewood that he anonymously gives to an elderly widow in his village.

Nevertheless, when asked to indicate whether an ethics course should focus more on difficult cases requiring rigorous decision-making or on edifying examples of virtuous moral character, astute students typically respond, "Both." The tough cases are needed for the first two ethics teaching aims and exemplary examples best promote the aim of moral character development.

Although cases, including those in this book, tend to focus on negative examples, positive examples are important as well. The latter do occur, but they are far too often unsung. For example, in July 1954, after a cheating scandal involving student athletes, the trustees of Washington & Lee University made a very controversial decision to replace its subsidized athletic program with an unsubsidized one. Loud and vigorous criticism rang through the land from alumni and sports writers

(Crenshaw, 1969, p. 350), but Dean James Leyburn led a courageous stand to preserve the student honor code. Ever since, Washington & Lee is usually missing from the national sports highlights—but its honor code remains in force. Another uplifting example, even less well known, is that of the dignified and gracious manner in which Dr. Owen Elder, executive vice president and dean of academics at a Christian college in the late 1980s, conducted himself honorably after he was pressured to step down to save money during a time of financial difficulty for the college. Readers can probably recall other exemplary cases from their own experiences. Perhaps they have been inspired and motivated to seek higher standards for themselves, just as this author has personally been by the above examples. Additional positive leadership outcomes are featured in Karen Longman's (2012) *Thriving in Leadership*. Administrators and faculty should relate such positive cases to newer generations, showing that there indeed is light from (as well for) the dark side.

In spite of the above qualifications, discussion of the cases in this book can raise sensitivity to ethical issues and the importance of applying rational thinking to challenging decision-making situations. Enlightened discussion can also suggest character development needs. Whereas moral character is a complex subject, responsible humans should seek character growth (2 Pet. 1:4-9). This applies to and is achievable by adults (Rest et al., 1986; Rest, 1986).

Case analysis is a useful way to promote character development. Other ways include observation and experience, reading inspirational and edifying literature, action learning involving dealing with difficult challenges in a variety of situations, role playing, deft application of praise, one-on-one mentoring, and explanatory use of didactic methods. There is no simple formula, but Christian administrators and faculty can and should prayerfully seek to further the ethical culture of their institutions as well as to grow as moral leaders (Whetstone, 2017).

The cases and essays of this volume are intended to contribute to an illumination of the dark side. Effective realization of this aim, of course, will come only through the working of the Holy Spirit on our minds, wills, and hearts.

References

Aeschliman, M. D. (2007). Virtue's aristocrat. *National Review*. (April 2), 46-47, 51.

Badaracco, J. L. (1995). *Business ethics: Roles and responsibilities*. Chicago, IL: Irwin.

Banks, R., & B. M. Ledbetter. (2004). *Reviewing leadership*. Grand Rapids, MI: Baker.

Beabout, G. (2012). Management as a domain-relative practice that requires and develops practical wisdom. *Business Ethics Quarterly*. 22: 405-432.

Berenbeim, R. E. (2007). Ethical leadership: Maintain an ethical culture. In J.E. Richardson, ed., *Annual editions: Business ethics 07/08*. McGraw-Hill.

Blanchard, K., & N. V. Peale. (1988). *The Power of Ethical Management*. NY: Fawcett Crest.

Butler, J. (1726). Upon self-deceit. *Fifteen sermons upon human nature*. In C. Sommers & F. Sommers. (2001). *Vice and virtue in everyday life*. Fort Worth, TX: Harcourt College Publishers, 397-403.

Carroll, A. B., & R. W. Scherer. (2003). *Vital speeches of the day*, 59:17, 529-533. In J. E. Richardson, ed. (2005). *Annual editions: Business ethics*, 17th ed. Dubuque, IA: McGraw-Hill/Duskin.

Chewning, R. C., J. W. Eby, and S. J. Roels. (1990). *Business through the eyes of faith*. San Francisco, CA: HarperSanFrancisco.

Ciulla, J. (2004). *Ethics, the heart of leadership*, 2nd ed. Westport, CT: Praeger.

Collins, J. (2001). *Good to great: Why some companies make the leap—and others don't*. NY: HarperBusiness.

Crenshaw, O. (1969). *General Lee's college: The rise and growth of Washington and Lee University*. NY: Random House.

Curren, R. (2010). Cardinal virtues of academic administration. In Englehardt et al., eds., 63-86.

DeGeorge, R. T. (2006). *Business ethics* (6th ed.). Upper Saddle River, NJ: Pearson Prentice Hall.

Derry, R. (1991). Institutionalizing ethical motivation: Reflections on Goodpaster's agenda. In R. Edward Freeman, ed. *Business ethics: The state of the art*. NY: Oxford University Press, 121-136.

Donovan, A. (2010). Mission and academic administration. In Englehardt et al., eds., 87-98.

Duska, R., & J. A. Ragatz. (2008). How losing soul leads to ethical corruption in business. In G. Flynn, ed. *Leadership and business ethics*. Springer, 151-163.

Englehardt, E. E., M. S. Pritchard, K. D. Romesburg, & B. E. Schrag, eds. (2010). *The ethical challenges of academic administration*. Dordrecht, The Netherlands: Springer.

Englehardt, E. E. (2010). Academic ethics in higher education administration: The dimensions of decisions. In Englehardt et al., eds., 13-24.

Garvin, D. (1993). Building a learning organization. *Harvard Business Review*. (July-August), 78-91.

Gert, B. (2004). *Common morality: Deciding what to do*. NY: Oxford Press.

Gunsalus, C. K. (2006). *The college administrator's survival guide*. Cambridge, MA.: Harvard University Press.

Holmes, A. (1984). *Ethics: Approaching moral decisions*. Downers Grove, IL: InterVarsity.

Jennings, M. M. (1999). *Business ethics: Case studies and selected readings,* 3rd ed. West.

Kennedy, S. (2018). Berkeley blues: An anatomy of institutional decay in California. *The American Conservative.* (January-February), 26-32.

Kline, D. (2010). On telling faculty the truth. In Englehardt et al., eds., 143-150.

Kohlberg, L. (1981). The child as a moral philosopher. In C. Sommers, & F. Sommers. (2001). *Vice & virtue in everyday life.* Fort Worth, TX: Harcourt, 579-603.

Kouzes, J., & B. Posner. (2003). *Credibility: How leaders gain and lose it, why people demand it.* San Francisco, CA: Jossey-Bass.

Longman, K., ed. (2012). *Thriving in leadership: Strategies for making a difference in Christian higher education.* Abilene, TX: Abilene Christian University Press.

Loui, M. C. (2010). How should policy apply? Trustworthy decisions in the administration of graduate academic programs. In Englehardt et al., eds., 135-141.

March, J. & H. Simon. (1993). *Organizations,* 2nd ed. Cambridge, MA: Blackwell.

March, J. (1994). *A Primer on decision-making: How decisions happen.* NY: Free Press.

Markkula Center for Applied Ethics under the direction of Manuel Velasquez. Web site: (www.scu.edu/ethics/practicing/decision/framework.html).

McFall, T. R. (2003). *Transformation ethics: Developing the Christian moral imagination.* Lanham, MD: University Press of America.

Newton, L. H. (2010). Educated warfare: Adversary relations in the groves of academe. In Englehardt et al., eds., 99-113.

Paine, L. S. (1994). Managing for organizational integrity. *Harvard Business Review.* 72:2, 106-117.

Paine, L. S. (2003). *Value shift: Why companies must merge social and financial imperatives to achieve superior performance.* NY: McGraw-Hill.

Plato. (1974). *The republic,* 2nd ed. Translated by Desmond Lee. London: Penguin.

Pritchard, M. S. (2010). Caught in the middle: On chairing a department. In Englehardt et al., eds., 49-62.

Rest, J. (1988). Can ethics be taught in professional schools? The psychological research. *Ethics: Easier Said Than Done*. 1, 22-26.

Rest, J., R. Barnett, M. Bebeau, D. Deemer, I. Getz, Y. Moon, J. Spickelmier, S. Thomas, & J. Volker. (1986). *Moral development: Advances in research and theory*. NY: Praeger.

Romesburg, K. D. (2010). Ethical dimensions of presidential leadership. In Englehardt et al., eds., 1-11.

Sanders, J. O. (1980). *Spiritual leadership*. Chicago, IL: Moody Press.

Schrag, B. E. (2010). Through the looking glass: Ethics and academic administration. In Englehardt et al., eds., 25-36.

Shaw, W. H. (2005) *Business ethics*, 5th ed. Belmont, CA: Thomson Wadsworth.

Sibbes, R. (1862). *Works*. Edinburgh: James Nichol.

Sison, A. J. G. (2006). Leadership, character and virtues from an Aristotelian viewpoint. In T. Maak & N. M. Pless, eds. *Responsible leadership*. London: Routledge, 108-121.

Smith, F. (1986). *Learning to lead*. Waco, TX: Word Books.

Sommers, C. (1991). Teaching the virtues. In C. Sommers & F. Sommers. (2001). *Vice & virtue in everyday life*. Fort Worth, TX: Harcourt College Publishers, 670-681.

Tocqueville, A. de. (1969). *Democracy in America*. Edited by J. P. Mayer and translated by G. Lawrence. NY: Harper & Row.

Weaver, G. R. (2017). Organizations and the development of virtue. In A. J. G. Sison, G. R. Beabout, & I. Ferrero, eds. (2017). *Handbook of virtue ethics in business and management*, vol 1. Dordrecht: Springer Science + Business Media, 613-622.

Weingartner, R. H. (1999). *The moral dimensions of academic administration*. Lanham, MD: Rowan & Littlefield Publishers, Inc.

Werhane, P. (1993). Letter to the editor. *Harvard Business Review*. 71 (November-December), 198.

Werhane, P. (1999). *Moral imagination and management decision-making*. NY: Oxford University Press.

Werner, D. (2010). On the dark side: Lessons learned as interim dean. In Englehardt et al., eds., 37- 47.

Whetstone, J. T. (2001). How virtue fits within business ethics. *Journal of Business Ethics*. 33:2, 101-114.

Whetstone, J. T. (2003). The language of managerial excellence: Virtues as understood and applied. *Journal of Business Ethics*. 44:3, 343-357.

Whetstone, J. T. (2005a). Choice of an executive assistant. *Journal of Biblical Integration and Business, Special Issue: Business Cases with a Christian Worldview*. Christian Business Faculty Association, 65-67.

Whetstone, J. T. (2005b). A framework for organizational virtue: The interrelationship of mission, culture, and leadership. *Business Ethics: A European Review*, 14:4, 367-378.

Whetstone, J. T. (2006). *The manager as a moral person: Exploring paths to excellence*. Charlotte, NC: Catawba.

Whetstone, J. T. (2013). *Leadership ethics & spirituality: A Christian perspective*. Bloomington, IN: WestBow/Thomas Nelson.

Whetstone, J. T. (2017). Developing a virtuous organizational culture. In A. J. G. Sison, G. R. Beabout, & I. Ferrero, eds. (2017). *Handbook of virtue ethics in business and management*, vol 1. Dordrecht: Springer Science + Business Media, 623-634.

About the Author

Dr. Whetstone earned degrees at Washington & Lee University, MIT, Reformed Theological Seminary, and the University of Oxford (D.Phil.). He has published numerous journal articles; his most recent book is a 2019 revised edition of his *Leadership Ethics & Spirituality*. An international scholar on applying virtue ethics in business, he has worked in corporate management, church ministry, university teaching and administration, and academic research and writing. Married with one son, he devotes his time to writing, speaking, reviewing for academic journals, and leadership of several civic organizations.